Good morning

~ M.M.

M000205537

H. NORMAN WRIGHT

Quiet Times

Times

for Every Parent

HARVEST HOUSE PUBLISHERS

EUGENE, OREGON

Cover by Dugan Design Group, Bloomington, Minnesota

Cover photo © Fresh Start Images / Alamy

QUIET TIMES FOR EVERY PARENT
Adapted from *Quiet Times for Parents*
Copyright © 1996/2010 by H. Norman Wright
Published by Harvest House Publishers
Eugene, Oregon 97402
www.harvesthousepublishers.com

ISBN 978-0-7369-2278-4

Printed in China

10 11 12 13 14 15 16 17 18 / RDS-NI / 10 9 8 7 6 5 4 3 2 1

Do not be anxious about anything, but in
everything, by prayer and petition, with thanksgiving,
present your requests to God *(Philippians 4:6)*.

❧

I t's been one of those days. Hectic, hurried, and hassled.
If you stopped for a minute, you would have been run
over. They were all right behind you waiting for you to
stumble—deadlines, dishes, the dentist, duties waiting
to devour you if you dallied just for a moment. It seemed
that everyone and everything, from the kids to the endless phone interruptions, wanted a piece of you.

Hurrying isn't the answer. That will stress you out more
and build panic. What you want to do is slow down. Why
not pray the following prayer by Charles Swindoll?

> [Lord,] steady my hurried pace with a vision
> of the eternal reach of time. Give me, amid
> the confusion of the day, the calmness of
> the everlasting hills…Slow me down, Lord,
> and inspire me to send my roots deep into
> the soil of life's enduring values, that I may
> grow toward my greater destiny.[1]

He who has a glad heart has a continual feast
[regardless of circumstances] *(Proverbs 15:15 AMP)*.

～

Laugh a little. No, laugh a lot. Those are words of wisdom. Laughter is one of God's gifts. Life is filled with incidents that lend themselves to not just a snicker, but an uncontrolled siege of laughter.

What's the laughter level in your family? As a parent, your children will supply you with many opportunities to laugh. Some of the time you may wonder if you should be laughing...or even wish you hadn't. Sometimes your kids misbehave in ways that are highly punctuated with something funny, and you end up desperately trying to keep a straight face while you correct them. We've all been through this dilemma.

A sense of humor reflects a healthy atmosphere within your home. When you laugh as a family, remember to laugh *with* one another rather than at one another. Look for the lighter side in the seriousness of life. This helps make parenthood a bit easier.

You are not your own; you were bought
at a price *(1 Corinthians 6:19-20)*.

Years ago a Christian publishing house came out with
a ministry to help prospective parents. It was called
"The Cradle Roll Program." This program provided written materials to assist parents who were preparing for
their child. The title of the material was called "Loan of
a Life," which reflected the fact that children don't really
belong to us. They're not our possessions. We've been
entrusted with their care and, in the natural progression
of life, they will be relinquished at a given point in time
to form their own families.

> To relinquish your children does not mean
> to abandon them, however. It means to give
> them back to God, and in so doing to take
> your hands off. It means neither to neglect
> your responsibilities toward them nor to
> relinquish the authority you need to fulfill
> those responsibilities. It means to release
> those controls that arise from needless fears
> or from selfish ambitions.[2]

> Train up a child in the way he should go [and in
> keeping with his individual gift or bent], and when he
> is old he will not depart from it *(Proverbs 22:6 AMP)*.

What does Proverbs 22:6 tell us about parenting? It explains the parental responsibility to dedicate our children to God and train them in His ways. In the original Hebrew text, the phrase "in the way he should go" reflects the thought that parents need to consider the particular child's stage of development and unique personality.

If you follow the advice in this proverb, there's a good probability that your children will either remain true to this instruction all their lives or return to God's teachings as they mature. Remember, though, that this is only a *probability,* not a certainty. What's important is that you understand the uniqueness of each child's personality and adapt your responses to that uniqueness. When you do that, you'll find yourself relaxing and becoming less frustrated. Isn't that another good reason to adapt to your children?

If anyone does not provide for his relatives, and especially for his immediate family, he has denied the faith and is worse than an unbeliever *(1 Timothy 5:8).*

Much is said about what we leave for our children through our wills and living trusts. At one time or another, everyone has to consider what will be left to his or her children when he or she dies. But you will leave more than that. You have passed on your genes as well. There is a biological pattern that was transferred to each child. There is also an emotional pattern that is being passed on from you to them, just as it was passed on to you from your parents. All of this is your legacy.

You're making an impact—an imprint on your children's lives. Most parents want to be positive role models for their children. Talk with your spouse or someone you love about how you want to raise your children. What rare experiences can you create for your children that would not only be a terrific memory, but also change their lives for the better?

A good name is to be more desired than great wealth,
favor is better than silver and gold (*Proverbs 22:1 NASB*).

~ ✠ ~

A daughter wrote this poem about her dad. It's a tribute
that all dads would like to have said about them.

Dad

Dad, you gave me life; the family name to
hold. You taught me humble pride and purity,
fine as gold.

Dad, you gave me love; you always held
my hand. You gave me trusting faith that in
hard times will stand.

Dad, you gave me strength; you showed
me how to smile. You were my constant friend
down many a weary mile.

Dad, you are my tower; you hold a special
place. When walking in your footsteps, there
I see your noble face.

Dad, you were a godly man; you taught
me how to pray, to love the Lord forever; His
Word will light the way.

Dad, many years have passed away since
you said "good-bye" to me.

I'll look for you in heaven, where we'll
spend eternity![3]

The prayer of a righteous man is powerful
and effective *(James 5:16)*.

❧

Do you have any special family traditions? These can include what you do for holidays, birthdays, vacations, mealtimes, the way you greet one another, and the way you say goodnight.

Take a moment and respond to the following questions.

1. What were the family traditions you experienced while growing up?

2. Which family traditions did you bring with you into your current family?

3. What new family traditions have you created?

4. What family traditions did your children's other parent bring?

5. What are the purposes and values of your family traditions?

What new tradition would you like to create? Perhaps it's the selection of a Scripture for the week that you all commit yourselves to follow. Or maybe it's telling each family member, "I prayed for you today."

My son, pay attention to my wisdom, listen well to my words of insight, that you may maintain discretion and your lips may preserve knowledge *(Proverbs 5:1-2)*.

W hat's a dad to do? That's the question many fathers ask, not just in the early years of parenting but all the way through. Often it's a question asked quietly and silently inside their hearts and minds. Here are some guidelines worth considering.

> The effective father recognizes that fatherhood is a mandate from God, and he accepts the responsibilities and privileges it brings. He makes a major investment of his time and energy in this calling. He knows that the God who called him to this unique ministry will sustain him through it.
>
> In his book *The Effective Father,* Gordon MacDonald uses the analogy of an orchestra conductor to describe the father's pacesetting role. In the analogy, the father is the conductor, his family is the orchestra, and God is the composer of the music. The father's task is to make sure the "orchestra" plays the music the way the "composer" wrote it.[4]

I press on toward the goal to win the prize
for which God has called me heavenward
in Christ Jesus *(Philippians 3:14)*.

Have you had days when you wanted to resign from your family? Probably! Totally overwhelmed by the ongoing battle, you're tempted to just give up trying so hard. Children feel that way at times. So do parents… and spouses…and siblings…and even grandparents. When everything falls apart, we all have those fleeting thoughts—and sometimes lasting ones too. Sometimes we don't even *like* the other people, even though we still *love* them. Our efforts will not always be recognized, appreciated, or even liked. Parenting is definitely not a popularity contest. If it were, we would lose much of the time.

It's reassuring, though, to know we don't have to be popular. We don't have to be a super parent. We don't have to compare ourselves with other parents. We just have to be faithful…and rely on the Lord.

May God give you of heaven's dew and
of earth's richness *(Genesis 27:28)*.

❧

I n the Old Testament you will find several occasions
when fathers blessed their children. These blessings
signified acceptance, which is foundational to building
self-esteem. Blessing your children will bolster their self-
image and help solidify their unique identities.

In their book *The Blessing,* Gary Smalley and John
Trent suggest five elements that constitute a blessing. The
first is *meaningful touch.* Studies show that loving touches
greatly enhance physical and emotional health.

Second, blessing may be bestowed through *spoken
words*—words of love, affirmation, and acceptance.

The third element of a blessing is *expressing high value.*
Recognize your children as special people and commu-
nicate this through your words.

The fourth element is *picturing a special future.* Do
your children feel hopeful or discouraged by your messages to them about what lies ahead?

The final element of a blessing is an *active commitment*
from you as a parent to do everything you can to help
your children fulfill their potential.[5]

> We have different gifts, according to the grace
> given us. If a man's gift is prophesying, let him
> use it in proportion to his faith *(Romans 12:6)*.

Take heart! There are many different styles of parenting. You don't have to be a replica of all the other parents you've known. God wants you to have the freedom to express your unique personality and spiritual gifts in your parenting (even if you're different from your life partner).

Let's consider for a moment how your spiritual gifts may be reflected in your parenting style. Romans 12:6 says, "We have different gifts, according to the grace given us." The word *gift* in the original Greek text is *charisma*. The root of this word means "joy" or "gladness." The seven gifts—prophesying, serving, teaching, encouraging, giving, leadership, mercy—described in Romans 12:6-8 are gifts of joy. So if you're aware of your gift and use it, the result is that you will be a person who brings joy and gladness to those around you. And remember, your gift is just that—a gift from God.[6]

May the grace of the Lord Jesus Christ, and the
love of God, and the fellowship of the Holy
Spirit be with you all *(2 Corinthians 13:14).*

A t the conclusion of a church service, just before you
leave, the pastor usually starts speaking again—
not to continue the sermon but to close with a few words
called "the benediction." Benedictions used to be passages
of Scripture, although today you may hear just about anything. Today's Scripture verse is a benediction. Another
common one is:

> May the God of peace, who through the
> blood of the eternal covenant brought back
> from the dead our Lord Jesus, that great
> Shepherd of the sheep, equip you with
> everything good for doing his will, and
> may he work in us what is pleasing to him,
> through Jesus Christ, to whom be glory for
> ever and ever. Amen (Hebrews 13:20-21).

These benedictions remind you that you're not going
through the week or even the day alone. Jesus Christ is
with you always.

A wise man's heart guides his mouth, and his
lips promote instruction *(Proverbs 16:23)*.

Our bodies are works of art (remember, beauty is in
the eye of the beholder!). Each body has a vast array
of different organs with varied purposes. One of them we
can't do without is the heart. Many people today suffer
from heart problems. This is the era of angiograms; angio-
plasty; single, double, triple, and quadruple bypasses; and
even heart transplants.

Is your heart free from trouble? A troubled heart lacks
peace and calm assurance. Some days this is reflected by
unrest, uncertainty, discontentment, and an inner churn-
ing. Troubled hearts come in many forms:

> *The heavy heart:* "An anxious heart weighs a
> man down, but a kind word cheers him up"
> (Proverbs 12:25).
>
> *The sorrowful heart:* "Even in laughter the heart
> may ache, and joy may end in grief" (Prov-
> erbs 14:13).

Do you or your children ever experience a troubled
heart? Use your ears. Listen with your eyes too. Let God
be the source of your thoughts, words, and actions. He
can comfort and change troubled hearts.[7]

Wait for the LORD; be strong and take heart
and wait for the LORD *(Psalm 27:14).*

❧

A favorite admonition of parents is "Wait!" It comes
in several formats: "Now you wait right there until
I tell you to move," "Now just wait! It's too close to din-
nertime for you to snack," or "Wait—wait—wait! You're
doing that all wrong!"

You may feel as if your entire life is made up of waiting.
You wait in line at the store, at the traffic signal, for the
child or spouse who is late, for the delivery. Isn't anyone
on time anymore? You hurry to your doctor's appoint-
ment and you end up—you guessed it—waiting! And
waiting seems like such a waste of time. Sometimes it
is—but there is one exception: waiting on God.

If you're a parent of prayer, you know that sometimes
you need to wait on God for your prayers to be answered.
Your strength will come from Him, and it will come
during the difficult time, not after.[8]

Then he said, "This is what I'll do. I will tear down
my barns and build bigger ones, and there I will
store all my grain and my goods" *(Luke 12:18).*

P ossessions—this is what life is all about for many
people. Ken Gire helps us put this in perspective with
this prayer:

Dear Teacher,

Teach me what life is all about. Help me
to learn that it does not consist of possessions,
no matter how many. Help me to realize that
the more things I selfishly accumulate, the
more barns I will have to build to store them
in. Help me to realize, too, that the storage fee
on such things is subtracted from a life that
could be rich toward you instead.

Teach me that life is more than the things
necessary to sustain it. Help me to learn that if
life is more than food, surely it is more important than how the dining room looks; it's more
than clothes, certainly it is more important
than whether there's enough closet space to
hold them.[9]

The Lord gives skillful and godly Wisdom;
from His mouth come knowledge and
understanding *(Proverbs 2:6 AMP)*.

❧

Parenting is a job, a vocation, a calling, a profession, a career. Here are three key components that will help keep you on track.

- *Agility.* This doesn't necessarily mean the ability to navigate the stairs with a load of wash, tiptoeing around the toys and shoes strewn in your way. Rather, it's the ability to respond in a productive way quickly and resourcefully.

- *Anticipation.* This is simply thinking in a futuristic way. It's not that you're controlled by the future. Rather, you're preparing for it even though you may not have all the information you need.

- *Adaptability.* This is the ability to flex and be versatile. You're capable of trying something different instead of entrenching yourself in the same old ruts.[10]

Get rid of all bitterness, rage and anger, brawling and
slander, along with every form of malice. Be kind and
compassionate to one another, forgiving each other,
just as in Christ God forgave you *(Ephesians 4:31-32)*.

❧

In today's verses we find a vocabulary test for parents.
Please take a moment to define these words: bitterness,
wrath, anger, evil speaking, and forgiveness. Better yet,
ask your children and your spouse for their definitions
too. Here are a few examples.

- *Bitterness* is a feeling of deep resentment
  and ill will toward another person.
- *Wrath* is an uncontrolled temper.
- *Anger* is a strong feeling of irritation.
- *Evil speaking* can include verbal abuse or
  slander that damages the reputation of
  other people (even family members).

None of these words reflect the presence of Jesus Christ
in the family. Here is one more definition:

- *Forgiveness* is taking an eraser and wiping
  the slate so clean it's as though the infrac-
  tion never—*never!*—occurred. Isn't that
  what God has done for us?

[He whose gift is] practical service, let him
give himself to serving; he who teaches, to
his teaching *(Romans 12:7 AMP)*.

A person whose gift is serving is devoted to meeting
the needs of others. In fact, some people who have
this gift seem to anticipate and care for people's needs
even before they are evident. This is actually the gift
of practical service. It's true that all parents will reflect
some aspect of this gift, but for some their entire lives
are devoted to this calling.

A child raised by a parent who has this gift will see
cheerfulness on display when his needs are met. This
parent engages in a great amount of teaching that's usually
done by showing and demonstrating rather than telling.
The parent may verbalize his instructions, but *doing* is
his or her forte.

All of us need to be givers in some way. This is the calling to everyone who claims Jesus as Lord of his or her life.[11]
How can you demonstrate giving in a new way today?

Let your tears flow like a river day
and night *(Lamentations 2:18)*.

~~~

Parents are guardians. You've been entrusted with the care, cultivation, and nurturing of delicate creations called children. The younger the child, the more fragile he or she is. The emotions children experience are wild, untamed, not understood, and need to be guided and shaped.

> God has given His children two precious but fragile gifts. Cupped within our emotions, these gifts bubble up or spill out as needed. Their names are laughter and tears. Both are wonderful friends to the poised person. They can be enjoyed privately or given as an investment in others…
>
> Tears are friends. Allies. Like the valve on top of a pressure cooker, they relieve the soul. Like laughter, they can soothe and medicate a broken heart…A loving home needs to be bathed in laughter, with parents setting the pace.[12]

That's right. You are the pacesetter. So let your tears flow when they need to, and laugh as often as possible.

> Train up a child in the way he should go [and in
> keeping with his individual gift or bent], and when he
> is old he will not depart from it *(Proverbs 22:6 AMP)*.

W hether you know it or not, you're a risk taker. Yes,
you really are. If you're a parent, you've got to be
a risk taker. Every day you face new changes and challenges. When you have a child your life changes forever.
Most parents don't know all the changes involved, or
if they have an inkling, they don't adequately prepare
for them.

One of the most frequently asked questions by parents
is, "What do I do now?" Many parents creep along the
path of uncertainty, never quite sure that what they're
doing is right—but hoping and praying it is.

Talk with your children. Be transparent. Share how
you are attempting to grow and change. Use Scripture
together as your model for living. It will lower the risk
factor.[13]

[Jesus] said: "I tell you the truth, unless you change and become like little children, you will never enter the kingdom of heaven" *(Matthew 18:3).*

Parents do a lot of teaching. It's a constant calling and challenge. But even as you teach your children, you're also being taught *by* your children. What can you learn?

- A child can teach you to be in awe over something that has become commonplace in your life.

- A child can teach you about faith and trust in Jesus as he or she prays for a sick puppy or for a friend to like him or her again.

- A child can teach you the wonder of being inquisitive when he or she bombards you with questions in an endless search to know.

- A child can teach you how to love and express your love without inhibitions or reservations.

- A child can teach you…

Why don't you finish that last sentence? What are your children teaching you?

I bow my knees before the Father of our Lord Jesus Christ, for Whom every family in heaven and on earth is named *(Ephesians 3:14-15 AMP)*.

W̲hat is a family? Can you answer that question with one word, a phrase, or a paragraph? Everyone has his or her own thoughts about what a family is, and sometimes the response varies depending on the day, the time, and the current behavior of the children. Think about this: What is a family? A family is a mobile. A family is an art form. A family is an exciting art career because an art form needs work.

> God's mobile—a human being—two human beings—a family of human beings. Mobiles that can reproduce. Constantly changing patterns, affected by each other, inspired by each other, helped by each other...A family is a blending of people for whom a career of making a shelter in the time of storm is worth a lifetime![14]

That's quite a bit to digest, isn't it? But what a difference it makes when our own family reflects this.

Only be careful, and watch yourselves closely so
that you do not forget the things your eyes have
seen or let them slip from your heart as long
as you live. Teach them to your children and to
their children after them (*Deuteronomy 4:9*).

P atrick Morley shares an interesting approach he and
his wife used to encourage their children to develop
a personal devotional life.

> Patsy and I offered our children a deal. "If you
> will do a daily devotion for at least twenty-five
> days each month, we'll buy you a...compact
> disc...In addition, if you do your devotions at
> least twenty-five days each month for ten out
> of twelve months we'll pay you $250."...
>
> At the end of the first year both children...
> had a perfect record of 365 days. They are well
> on their way to establishing a spiritual disci-
> pline which can keep them close to their Lord
> all their days. Some might call it bribery. I like
> to think of it as giving our children what they
> *need* in the context of what they *want*.[15]

God demonstrates his own love for us in this: While
we were still sinners, Christ died for us *(Romans 5:8)*.

～

Fathers. They come in all sizes, strengths, tempera-
ments, and abilities. And many of them, when they
were children, began to fashion their understanding of
God based on their own fathers. For some of us, that was
good. But for others, that wasn't so good.

Rather than base our beliefs upon a human father,
it's better to look to Scripture to understand who God
is. He is…

- the loving, concerned Father who is interested
  in the intimate details of our lives (Matthew
  6:25-34).
- the Father who never gives up on us (Luke 15:3-
  32).
- the God who sent His Son to die (Romans 5:8).
- available to us through prayer (John 14:13-14).
- aware of our needs (Isaiah 65:24).
- for us (Romans 8:31).
- a God of hope (Romans 15:13).
- a God who wants us to be free (Galatians 5:1).
- someone who values us (Matthew 10:29-31).
- our Comforter (2 Corinthians 1:3-5).

Each of us has one body with many
members, and these members do not all
have the same function *(Romans 12:4)*.

⁓

A few days ago I asked, What is a family? It's important for your children to have a positive regard for
your family. Why? This is the first place where children
learn to love. It's your children's launching pad into the
big outdoors. As your children participate in your family,
they experience the diversity of life without having to
bear full responsibility for what happens. Family is a
place of joy and sadness, a place to learn to take and share
responsibility, a place to express feelings and discover a
positive identity.

> A family is a well-regulated hospital, a nurs-
> ing home, a shelter in time of physical need,
> a place where a sick person is greeted as a
> sick human being and not as a machine
> that has a loose bolt or a mechanical doll
> that no longer works.[16]

He who covers and forgives an offense seeks
love, but he who repeats or harps on a matter
separates even close friends (*Proverbs 17:9 AMP*).

~&~

To a Child About to Be Married

After you've married, a day will come when you will
need to practice one of the elements of God's grace
to all of us—forgiveness. I'd like to be honest with you:
Some days you won't feel that your partner deserves your
forgiveness. That's all right. It's nothing new. None of us
deserve the forgiveness we receive.

Sometimes you may find it hard to forgive your spouse.
You may be concerned that by forgiving your partner
you're letting your mate off the hook and that what happened may reoccur. But, after all, the only other option
is resentment and revenge.

Forgiveness is also costly because when you forgive,
you're saying to your partner, "You don't have to make
up to me for what you did." You're actually releasing
your partner and reaching out in love instead of relishing resentments.

[I] beg you to walk (lead a life)…with complete
lowliness of mind (humility) and meekness
(unselfishness, gentleness, mildness), with patience,
bearing with one another and making allowances
because you love one another *(Ephesians 4:1-2 AMP)*.

❧

A family is comprised of several unique creations of God. All sizes, shapes, personalities, preferences, and metabolisms will be found under the same roof. Everyone has received gifts that need nourishment to bloom. A spouse becomes a gardener toward his or her partner as does a parent toward a child. As in any garden, the soil must be prepared and cultivated and each plant must be tended, protected, fed, watered, and given the ultimate in care.

A home is not a place where one person dominates or fashions the uniqueness of the others. When God's Word talks about "making allowances because you love one another," it means we are to be flexible and adapt to the differentness of each person. We are to learn to understand how each is different and then accept this differentness as part of God's creation.

Now if we are children, then we are heirs—
heirs of God and co-heirs with Christ, if indeed
we share in his sufferings in order that we
may also share in his glory *(Romans 8:17)*.

Your children could turn out to look just like you! That's right. They may have the same height, weight, build, eyes, hair (or lack of), nose, mouth—you name it, they may have or get it. They can become a mirror reflection made in your image (for better or for worse).

But both you and your children were created in another image—the image of God. That's what gives you and your child so much value! It's true the image was distorted by sin, but when you accept Christ as your Savior there is restoration.

Have you ever looked at your children and thought, *These kids were created in the image of God!* This puts them and their lives in a brand-new perspective, doesn't it? Pray that this will be seen in all they (and you) do.

All have sinned and fall short of the
glory of God *(Romans 3:23)*.

❧

As our children grow up, what do they need to know
about themselves so they have a balanced perspective on who they really are? We don't want them to turn
out conceited or proud, having an inflated view of who
they are. Nor do we want them to end up with a poor
perspective of their worth. So what is the message we
need to get across to them?

That's a good question. Here are three messages a child
needs to understand.

- First, children, just like their parents, are
  sinful.

- Second, children need to know they are
  wonderful. They were made in God's image
  and are unique, wondrous creations.

- Third, children need to experience acceptance—unconditional acceptance based on
  who they are, not what they do.

So…you, me, our children—we're a strange blend,
aren't we? Sinful, yes. Wonderful, yes. Accepted by God,
yes. That's a balanced view. Maybe it's not the world's view,
but that's okay. This view is much better![17]

Your will be done *(Matthew 6:10)*.

～⚮～

Parents want their children to obey them. It's good for the child and the parent. When a child doesn't obey, parents usually get upset. But it's not only children who disobey. Adults disobey as well. One area of disobedience is our resistance to the prayer, "[God,] Your will be done."

Oftentimes we're afraid of God's will. Why? Perhaps it's because we're not sure what His will is, and we wonder whether it's really best for us or not. Some of us are afraid that God will allow us to experience all the bad circumstances in life in order to discipline us. One major reason has to do with control. *We* want to be in control of our lives rather than surrender our wills to God, so it's a struggle to be obedient. But God already knows that, doesn't He?

"Your will be done" is a prayer that says, "God, You know what's best for me, and I know You want the best for me. I will trust You."

The memory of the righteous will
be a blessing *(Proverbs 10:7)*.

❧

Family memories are built on relationships, experiences, and the investment of time. Bart Campolo wrote this letter to his father, Tony:

> The times that I remember best are the times I spent with you. I love those memories best of all, Dad, and they're a big part of who I am. That's the whole point of these letters for me. My childhood is gone, and I will never be able to be with you the way I was with you as a little boy. I will never be that small, and you will never seem that big again…
>
> When you die, Dad, I will surely go to pieces for a while, because I still count on you more than anyone knows, but in the end I will be all right. I will have my stories, and in them I will always have part of you, the part that tells me who I am and where I came from.[18]

> Love, Bart

The prayer of a righteous man is powerful
and effective *(James 5:16)*.

⇜

P atrick Morley shares some of his prayer list for his
children...

- A saving faith (thanksgiving if already Christian)
- A growing faith
- An independent faith (as they grow up)
- Persevering faith
- A sense of destiny (purpose)
- A desire for integrity
- A call to excellence
- To understand their spiritual gifts
- To understand the ministry God has for them
- Values and beliefs, a Christian worldview
- To tithe and save 10 percent of all earnings
- To acquire wisdom
- The mate God has for them (alive somewhere, needing prayer)
- To do daily devotions
- Forgiveness and be filled with the Holy Spirit
- Glorify the Lord in everything

The prayers of righteous parents are both powerful and effective.[19]

God...gave [Jesus] the name that is
above every name *(Philippians 2:9)*.

～⌘～

Did you struggle over the names of your children?
Why did you select what you did? What do the
names signify? What do they mean? In the Scriptures,
names were sometimes changed to reflect or to signify a
new direction or even a new nature for the person involved.
Abram was changed to *Abraham* and *Jacob* to *Israel*. *Jacob*
meant "supplanter," but *Israel* meant that as a spiritual
prince, he had power with God. Jesus changed Simon's
name to *Peter,* which meant "rock."

The person who probably has more names than anyone
else is our Lord. Not only did God give Jesus "the name
that is above every name," He gave Him more than 100
names and titles throughout the Old and New Testaments. Why would He do that? No one name can be
used to adequately describe or define Jesus. Each name
and title reveals a unique aspect of who He is and what
His purposes are.

What's in a name? Everything.[20]

How long, O LORD? Will You forget me forever? How long will You hide Your face from me? *(Psalm 13:1 NASB).*

✦

Have you ever fallen flat on your face? Perhaps you know what it's like to be walking somewhere and suddenly trip and have your entire body hit the ground. You lie there with your nose either burrowed an inch deep or flattened against your face. That's one way to be flat on your face. But there is also another way.

David, the writer of the psalm referenced today, was flat on his face because he was despondent. He was down. He felt abandoned by God. Sound familiar? But David came to his senses. Instead of complaining and berating God, he went on to say, "Consider and answer me, O LORD, my God; enlighten my eyes" (verse 3 NASB). David doesn't see God as distant; he is asking God for an answer. David moved from being flat on his face to being on his knees. Have you been there lately? It's not that uncomfortable. Praying places problems in perspective.

The Lord said to Moses, "I will do the very thing
you have asked, because I am pleased with you
and I know you by name" *(Exodus 33:17).*

⤳

Why were you born? Is that a strange question? Perhaps—but who of us hasn't wondered? Obviously you are the product of your parents' involvement. But what else? Is there more to your existence than that? Yes! You were born to know God. That's why you're here.

As we journey through life learning to know God, we discover a wonderful truth: God knows us completely and loves us just as we are. He knows us through and through. He said to Jeremiah, "Before I formed you in the womb I knew you, before you were born I set you apart" (Jeremiah 1:5).

Perhaps the importance of being known by God is best expressed by J.I. Packer: "What matters supremely, therefore, is not, in the last analysis, the fact that I know God, but the larger fact which underlies it—the fact that *He knows me.*"[21]

Bless the LORD, O my soul *(Psalm 103:1 NASB)*.

❧

L et's bow our heads and ask God to bless this meal." Have you ever said that? What would you say if one of your children asked, "Why do we do this?" That's a good question. Do you have a good answer? Asking God to bless the meal is a way of acknowledging that He is the giver of life and the giver of gifts large and small. We're letting Him know that we realize we're dependent upon Him for everything.

Let's consider some creative steps you can take when you ask the blessing.

First, think before you pray. Create your prayer out of the reality of life itself.

Second, why not involve everyone in the prayer by asking for one- or two-sentence prayers?

Third, you could sing a brief hymn or the doxology. Or you could learn some sign language for a prayer or hymn and have everyone sign it.

And after the meal, why not ask everyone if they remember what was prayed for before the meal?

Jesus was in the stern, sleeping on a cushion. The
disciples woke him and said to him, "Teacher,
don't you care if we drown?" *(Mark 4:38).*

~~≈~~

Such an honest cry…a doggedly painful cry. I've asked
that one before, haven't you? It's been screamed count-
less times.

As the winds howled and the sea raged, the
impatient and frightened disciples screamed
their fear at the sleeping Jesus. "Teacher, don't
you care that we are about to die?" He could
have kept on sleeping. He could have told
them to shut up. He could have impatiently
jumped up and angrily dismissed the storm.
He could have pointed out their immaturity…
But he didn't.

With all the patience that only one who
cares can have, he answered the question. He
hushed the storm so the shivering disciples
wouldn't miss his response. Jesus answered
once and for all the aching dilemma of man,
Where is God when I hurt?

Listening and healing. That's where he is.
He cares.[22]

Discipline your son while there is
hope *(Proverbs 19:18 NASB).*

❧

For some parents, discipline means exasperation, hair pulling, and sleep-losing frustration. But it doesn't have to be that way. The word *discipline* means "to take action; to restrain or rectify the behavior of someone under you." Discipline is given to help someone improve or learn a lesson that will make him or her a better person.

Discipline *positively.* It's much more effective in child training to *encourage* and *reinforce good behavior* than to correct misbehavior. When you expect positive and healthy behavior, you're more likely to see it. It's been suggested that a 10-to-1 ratio in discipline is best. It's better to give 10 responses praising good behavior for every 1 response that corrects wrong behavior.

Expect the best and look for it. If on a given day 25 percent of the time your child behaved, talk more about that than the 75 percent of the time he or she misbehaved. You may find the percentages changing based on how you respond.[23]

Jesus said, "If you hold to my teaching, you are really my disciples. Then you will know the truth, and the truth will set you free" *(John 8:31-32)*.

～❧～

From time to time it's best just to stop, pray, and ask God for His strength in our lives. William Barclay's words voice what all of us need:

> O God, our Father, direct and control us in every part of our life.
>
> Control our tongues, that we may speak no false, no angry, no impure word.
>
> Control our actions, that we may do nothing to shame ourselves or to injure anyone else.
>
> Control our minds, that we may think no evil, no bitter, nor irreverent thought.
>
> Control our hearts, that they may never be set on any wrong thing, and that they may ever love only the highest and the best...
>
> This we ask for your love's sake. Amen.[24]

Commit your way to the LORD; trust in him *(Psalm 37:5)*.

⁓⊱⊰⁓

Sometimes parents are frustrated when they ask their child to do a task. They hear, "Oh, sure, I will," but nothing ever happens.

By the same token, sometimes children are frustrated when they make a request to their parents and get the same kind of response. It works both ways. Promises requested. Promises given. Promises broken. And the result? Lowered trust.

All of us want certainty. We want someone and something to depend on. We need security in the midst of an insecure world. We can't always depend on people. After all, we're marred because of the fall, and sometimes our actions don't match our words. There is One, however, who always delivers on what He says. God said, "Never will I leave you; never will I forsake you" (Hebrews 13:5). Jesus said, "Surely I am with you *always*, to the very end of the age" (Matthew 28:20). If God says He will, then He will!

Put on a heart of compassion *(Colossians 3:12 NASB)*.

❧

This is an interesting verse, but how does a person put on a heart of compassion? Is it a matter of developing new feelings? If so, how do we do that? True compassion is not just a feeling for another person. Nowhere in Scripture does it say to be compassionate or loving or kind "if you feel like it." The Bible says to do it. Compassion, as taught in the Scripture, is not expressed by feeling, but by action.

Who in your life needs a touch of compassion today? Perhaps someone needs a literal touch, such as a hug or a shoulder rub. Another type of touch could be a note in a lunch sack, a phone call of encouragement, or telling someone, "I want you to know that I will be praying for you today for that test [or sporting event or whatever]."

True compassion can be costly. It requires learning to care about what other people care about.

Children are a gift of the LORD *(Psalm 127:3 NASB)*.

❧

There are times when even the best of parents have mixed feelings about some of the gifts God has entrusted to them—their children. Sometimes kids don't seem like much of a gift, but they are. Your family can bring glory to God because of your children. How? God's Word indicates that children are a blessing just because they're gifts from God. They can glorify God as you lead them to a saving knowledge of Jesus Christ and see His character developed in them.

Not only can children be a glory to God, they also can help in your spiritual development. Married couples learn to bend, become flexible, and give up pockets of selfishness. The process begun in marriage is continued and deepened by the coming of children.

Yes, you will be inconvenienced, challenged, and made uncomfortable by your children. But rejoice! Their presence stretches you and causes you to learn in ways unknown to you before their arrival.[25]

If we confess our sins, he is faithful and just
and will forgive us our sins and purify us
from all unrighteousness *(1 John 1:9)*.

~~✦~~

Most of us don't feel guilty that often, yet some people go through their entire lives struggling with guilt. Guilt is a powerful emotion that can have a positive or negative effect on our lives. It can warn us of danger and motivate us to take corrective action. It can rob us of our joy or open the door to greater joy. It can distort our views or help us see things from God's perspective. We can allow guilt to keep us imprisoned in our pasts or let it serve as a motivator to learn and grow beyond our experiences.

Healthy guilt is constructive. It is an appropriate emotional response to the clear violation of a civil, spiritual, or relational standard. Healthy guilt is from God. Guilt is to our spirits what pain is to our bodies. It warns us when something is wrong and needs attention or correction.[26]

Cease striving and know that I am
God *(Psalm 46:10 NASB).*

Your kids have been on an outing all day. They chugged down Cokes, candy, and lots of chocolate. They played hard, and now it's evening. They're exhausted; you're exhausted. They're so exhausted they're running around shrieking, bouncing from wall to wall, totally out of control. And you've reached your limit. At the top of your voice you scream, "That's enough! Quiet!"

Suddenly there's a deathly calm. Everything comes to a halt. The only sound is silence. You spoke to your children, and they got the message.

As a parent, our Father God speaks to each of us. Have we gotten the message? He says to us in the midst of our chaos and panic, "Cease striving and know that I am God." The Hebrew word for "cease" means "relax, do nothing, be quiet." Are you saying, "I can't! There's too much to do"? God says, "It's okay. Take a break. Don't sweat it. Let Me handle your situation."

Can you refuse such an offer? It's for your good. God didn't design us to live at such a frantic pace.

Do not worry about tomorrow, for tomorrow
will worry about itself *(Matthew 6:34)*.

Y̶ou've been invited to the governor's mansion for a special reception and dinner a month from now. The surprise and excitement of the invitation is soon overshadowed by a very common concern: "What shall I wear?" The anticipatory delight is soon dampened by the concern over what rags to throw on for the evening.

Or let's say you've invited guests over for dinner. Is your concentration and energy directed toward the enjoyment and fellowship of the upcoming event? Or does a sense of panic rise as you ask, "What am I going to serve?" and "How can I get the house cleaned up in time?" These are legitimate questions to be asked and answered. But too often we let our concerns about the future drain our joy in the present.

Let God into your decision-making, your concerns, and your difficulties. Let Him have an opportunity to dispel your concerns, fill you with peace, and give you the ability to handle what you'll face today. Let go of tomorrow. It will be here soon enough.

I will do whatever you ask in my name, so that the
Son may bring glory to the Father. You may ask me for
anything in my name, and I will do it *(John 14:13-14)*.

⌇

Why do you pray? Go ahead—take a moment to
answer this question. Now, how would you answer
the question if it were put to you by a three-year-old? A
seven-year-old? A fifteen-year-old?

There are many reasons for praying. One is that praying
for other people brings us closer to them and also influences our attitudes toward them. Another reason is that
when we pray, we become much closer to God. It's our
way of communicating with Him. We didn't just learn
to do this; He created us for this purpose.

Yet another reason to pray is that God has resources
and blessings for us that we won't receive until we go to
Him in prayer.

Remember, prayer is not to change but to receive the
mind and will of God. Talking to God is not our idea;
it's His. We don't have to get His attention. He is waiting for our attention. Ask the Holy Spirit right now to
stir your spirit and create a greater hunger and thirst for
your heavenly Father.

Rejoice with those who rejoice; mourn with
those who mourn (*Romans 12:15*).

Carry each other's burdens, and in this way you
will fulfill the law of Christ (*Galatians 6:2*).

~~≈~~

S ome homes have an atmosphere that is pleasant, comfortable, and friendly. You know what it's like to enjoy
such a home. Some homes have an atmosphere that is
tense, on edge, uncomfortable, and strained. You probably know what that's like too. Have you ever wondered
what makes the difference? Think about this:

> Part of a family's function is to shoulder one
> end of our burdens and to share the delight
> of our blessings…Helping us to celebrate
> God's love is the chief blessing our families
> can give us…Only as we know how much
> God loves each of us can we begin to know
> how to love each other.[27]

God's love not only gives us eternal life with Him, but
it also makes life much better here when we allow it to
permeate our thoughts, feelings, and the way we respond
to one another. How can God's love be implemented to
impact your family life today?

Blessed are those who mourn, for they
will be comforted *(Matthew 5:4)*.

L oss. It's a simple four-letter word that is one of our
constant companions through life. And yet we don't
talk about it often. With each and every loss comes the
potential for change, growth, new insights, understanding, and refinement—all positive descriptions and words
of hope.

You may have faced many losses in your life already.
You may not even be aware of some of them or you may
not have realized that what you experienced were actually losses.

How you respond to your losses and what you let them
do to you can affect the rest of your life. You can't avoid
loss or shrug it off. Loss is not the enemy; not facing its
presence in our lives is.

God's Word tells us that loss produces maturity. The
character qualities of patience, endurance, humility, long-
suffering, gratitude, and self-control can also develop
through our losses. And when you experience loss, you
will discover the extent of God's comfort.[28]

My son, give attention to my words...for they are
life to those who find them (*Proverbs 4:20,22 NASB*).

～✦～

What makes a dad successful? What are the ingredients? For some answers, let's look at a young father who reflected on his dad. He believed that his father was an excellent example of what God requires and desires in fathers. Here is what he says:

1. Dad was always available.

2. My father made a sacrifice for me.

3. Dad was a man of consistency, who set a strong example.

4. My father's affection built lasting bonds of friendship. Dad never hesitated to reach out and hug me or pat me on the shoulder.

5. My father had a wife who loved and encouraged him.

6. Dad always expected the best of me. When Dad gave me a job or responsibility, he always assumed that I would carry it out to the best of my ability.

7. Dad loved me for who I was.

8. Dad was always proud of me.

9. Dad built memories for me.

10. My father learned early where his real priorities were.[29]

Then his father Isaac said to him, "Come
here, my son, and kiss me" *(Genesis 27:26).*

❧

Perhaps your children have asked you to come into their
rooms and rub their backs. They enjoy the relaxing
and soothing quality of your touch. Have you ever had
the opportunity to experience a full-hour body massage?
If so, you know the effect of touch on your muscles.

When people are apart for a long time and they meet
again, why do they touch or shake hands or embrace? It's
because the message conveyed by touch says much more
than words can. When your arms go around another
person at a time of loss you're speaking volumes whereas
words might not have been heard.

Have you noticed the difference in your child's response
when you say, "I love you," compared to saying, "I love
you," and touching him or her at the same time? Perhaps
touching makes our words more believable.[30]

He will be the sure foundation for your times, a rich
store of salvation and wisdom and knowledge; the fear
of the LORD is the key to this treasure *(Isaiah 33:6)*.

~⌇~

"Control! I want to be in control of my life!" All of
us have said that. But some people have taken this
desire to the extreme and have become controllers. You've
probably met them before.

People with rigid personalities, who are highly dom-
inating or perfectionists, have difficulty handling life
because they aren't flexible. Instead of being resilient, they
are brittle. The more unexpected the problem, the more
trouble they have. Setbacks cause them to make adjust-
ments and changes, and this causes them difficulty. In
addition to their rigidity, they lack a wide range of coping
skills, which exacerbates the problem.

What we all need to remember is this: We never *were*
in total control! We are not in total control now. We never
will be in total control. *God,* not us, is in control. Why
stay in bondage to the myth that we must be in control?
There is a better way to live.

The word of the LORD came to me, saying, "Before
I formed you in the womb I knew you, before
you were born I set you apart; I appointed you
as a prophet to the nations" *(Jeremiah 1:4-5).*

Does God create mistakes? That's a tough question. Think about it for a minute. Some of us do wonder about that. For example, have you ever wished your child's physical characteristics were different? What about your child's personality? Perhaps you're organized, structured, punctual, and bright and cheerful in the morning. But your child doesn't seem to have one drop of blood from your genes. Why did your child have to be that way? And some days you wonder about that more than others.

Jeremiah brings us back to an important fact. God said, "I made you." God created you and your child for a specific purpose. You may not be all that you wanted to be. Your child may not be what you expected. But you and your child are very important to God.

As the Father has life in himself, so he has granted
the Son to have life in himself *(John 5:26)*.

❧

I can do it myself. I don't need anyone's advice or help."
You've heard that before and perhaps have even said
it yourself. You're self-sufficient…or at least you think
so. Children say this much of the time in their eager-
ness to try new adventures or to let you know they're
growing up. This is the battle cry of the independent,
strong-willed child.

Fortunately, as we go through life we realize we aren't
self-sufficient. We don't know it all or have all the capa-
bilities we need—especially as parents. Something new
always seems to come up just when we think we've got
it all together.

You have needs. Your family has needs. We all have
needs. And part of our calling is to help meet each other's needs.

But God doesn't have any needs. He's different. But if
He is all-sufficient, where do we come in? That's simple:
Our holy God doesn't need us, but He *desires* us.[31]

Do not seek revenge or bear a grudge
against one of your people, but love your
neighbor as yourself *(Leviticus 19:18)*.

~⚜~

This is a message from one of America's favorite pastors, Max Lucado:

> A relationship. The delicate fusion of two human beings. The intricate weaving of two lives; two sets of moods, mentalities, and temperaments. Two intermingling hearts, both seeking solace and security.
>
> A relationship. It has more power than any nuclear bomb and more potential than any promising seed. Nothing will drive a man to a greater courage than a relationship.
>
> What matters most in life is not what ladders we climb or what possessions we accumulate. What matters most is a relationship.
>
> What steps are you taking to protect your "possessions"? What measure are you using to ensure that your relationships are strong and healthy? What are you doing to solidify the bridges between you and those in your world?
>
> Our Master knew the value of a relationship. It was through relationships that he changed the world.[32]

He will be called…Everlasting Father *(Isaiah 9:6)*.

～

Remember the day you were born? Hardly. Remember the day your child was born? Absolutely. How could you forget it? That was the beginning. You and your child had a beginning, and you will have an ending. Right now people refer to you and your child as "who you are." But one day that will change, and people will refer to you as "who you were" or say "Do you remember…?"

Many parents struggle over the future. They wish they could gaze ahead into the upcoming years and know either what's going to happen or how to control and determine future events. But that's impossible.

Every year as we get older, a bell goes off somewhere in the recesses of our minds to remind us there are fewer days remaining in our schedules. But remember, Jesus is in charge of time. He's the one who holds the future in His hands.[33]

[There is] a time to be silent and a
time to speak *(Ecclesiastes 3:7)*.

※

Communication—a family cannot exist without it.
No relationship can continue without interaction.
That's true not only between us and other people, but also
between us and God! Of all the books written on communication, the best and most practical resource is the
Word of God. Read the following verses and endeavor to
practice these biblical principles of communication even
more than you've been doing up to this point.

> Speaking the truth in love, we are to grow up
> in all aspects into Him who is the head, even
> Christ (Ephesians 4:15 NASB).

> He who conceals his sins does not prosper, but
> whoever confesses and renounces them finds
> mercy (Proverbs 28:13).

> Let him who wants to enjoy life and see good
> days...keep his tongue free from evil and
> his lips from guile (treachery, deceit) (1 Peter
> 3:10 AMP).

> There is one who speaks rashly like the thrusts
> of a sword, but the tongue of the wise brings
> healing (Proverbs 12:18 NASB).

Set your minds on things above, not
on earthly things *(Colossians 3:2).*

❧

Choices—life is full of them. You make choices all day long. For most of us some choices are good and others are not so good. And as a parent, you try to give your children the opportunity to make choices.

One choice is the decision to choose to be happy, content, and fulfilled. How is that possible with a house full of demanding children? Choose your attitude. You'll find it helpful to read the following out loud each morning for a week. Note the difference in your outlook.

> *Just for today* I will set my affection on things above, not on things on the earth.
>
> *Just for today* I will not worry about what will happen tomorrow, but will trust that God will go before me into the unknown.
>
> *Just for today* I will endure anything that hurts or depresses me because I believe God controls what happens to me.
>
> *Just for today* I will not dwell on my misfortunes. I will replace my negative thoughts with happy and hopeful thoughts.[34]

Do not withhold good from those who deserve
it, when it is in your power to act *(Proverbs 3:27).*

A t funerals and memorial services, oftentimes one or
more family members and friends will deliver eulogies. They share the positive qualities, characteristics, and
accomplishments of the deceased. They extol the person's
virtues and go into detail as to why the person will be
missed. Everyone present hears the kind and affirming
words except one—the person who is being talked about.
Sometimes you wonder if the person knew, while he or
she was alive, this was how people felt. You wonder how
much of what was shared in the eulogy was ever told to
the person directly when he or she was living. Perhaps
some of it was…or none of it.

So many parents and children end up saying about
loved ones, "If only I had told them how much I loved
them, what I appreciated, and how much they meant to
me." "If only" are words of regret and sadness over missed
opportunities. The presence of positive words can motivate, encourage, and lift up someone. So tell the people
you love how you feel.

Confess your sins to each other and pray for each
other so that you may be healed. The prayer of a
righteous man is powerful and effective *(James 5:16).*

~≈~

To love, accept, and respond to our children the way
God calls us to, we need to be refreshed by Him and
His grace. You might find it beneficial to pray this prayer
out loud each day for several weeks to allow the truths to
penetrate your heart and mind.

Prayer for Trust in the Spirit of God

I will not worry, fret or be unhappy over you.
I will not be afraid for you.
I will not blame you, criticize you or
   condemn you.
I will remember first, last and always
that you are God's child,
that you have his Spirit in you.
I will be patient with you,
I will stand by in faith
and bless you in my prayers,
knowing that you are growing,
knowing that you are finding the help
   you need.[35]

You are the light of the world *(Matthew 5:14)*.

There's a light shining from your house. You may not see it, but it's there. That light is you. Jesus said we are the light of the world. But what does that mean? A light has got to shine. A person who knows Jesus as Lord and Savior can't keep it to him- or herself. You can't be a private Christian.

It's as though Jesus was saying, "I've started something—a ministry to people. But I'm going back to the Father. So each of you needs to continue My ministry."

The first place we need to be a light is in our homes. Listen to what children who have seen their parents' light say about it:

> "My mom didn't only talk about her faith. I saw it in action."

> "Dad showed us what it meant to be a Christian by what he said, how he said it, and by what he didn't say. He was different from other men at home and at the factory."

Blessed are those who hunger and thirst for
righteousness, for they will be filled *(Matthew 5:6)*.

Most parents would like their children to be ambi-
tious. After all, isn't that the opposite of being lazy?
You want them to be industrious—to do the best they
can and achieve. There is nothing wrong with ambition.
But it's so easy for ambition to be misdirected.

What form should a parent's ambition take? Toward
what goal should we direct our children? Righteousness.
We're called to possess righteousness. The righteousness
of Christ was given to us when we accepted Him. We're
called to practice righteousness. Which means that what
we say, where we go, what we do, and who we spend time
with will be different. That, of course, will set a positive
example for our children.

We're also called to ambitiously promote righteousness—to do the right thing and work against the wrong
thing. That's a big task. But we don't have to do it in our
own strength. We have Jesus to help us![36]

Forgive us our debts, as we also have
forgiven our debtors *(Matthew 6:12)*.

✧

Years ago there was an old country song called "Sixteen Tons." It ends with "I owe my soul to the company store." Many people go through life owing everyone...or so it seems. Sometimes we'll receive a favor from someone and he or she will say, "You owe me." And with our children we sometimes feel like they owe us for all we've done for them.

Who do you owe? And what do you owe? There are many things we can owe other than money. Is there anyone to whom you owe a letter? Is there anyone to whom you owe an apology? What about owing someone a visit or a call or a bit of your time? And what do you owe yourself? A bit of solitude, time to sit and read, or lunch with a friend? Sometimes we're in debt to ourselves as much as to others.[37]

We have different gifts, according to the grace given
us…if it is teaching, let him teach *(Romans 12:6-7)*.

❧

Some parents instill within their children a quest for
knowledge and a thirst for learning. These parents
have been given the gift of teaching. It's true that all parents are to teach and will teach, but for some it's natural
and happens constantly.

Wise parents know the value or strength of their gifts as
well as the weakness of overusing gifts. When your child
asks the time, you don't tell him or her how the watch
or clock was made. A wise parent-teacher also allows for
individual differences within children and looks for teach-
able moments. And they work with their children to help
them discover their own uniqueness or giftedness.

All parents can and will teach. For some it's a natural ability with a joyful attitude. The gift you have will
be a blessing for your family. Discover your gift, rejoice
in it, and use it.[38]

Jesus answered, "Do you think that these Galileans
were worse sinners than all the other Galileans
because they suffered this way? I tell you, no! But
unless you repent, you too will all perish" *(Luke 13:2-3)*.

❧

J esus had some strong words for the crowd He was
talking with, but they're applicable for today as well.
Sometimes we think the reason bad things happen to
people is because those individuals deserved it. They
brought it on themselves. Sometimes that's true and
sometimes it's not.

When something bad happens to someone you don't
like, don't get along with, or compete against, how do
you respond inside? All of us have probably struggled
with this at one time or another. We have a tendency
to gloat silently. We may even feel gratified and justi-
fied over another person's misfortunes. That's easy to do
if it's obvious that person is wrong or has violated some
law. We think he or she deserves it.

But there's a better way to respond. It's found in 1 Corinthians 13:6: "Love does not delight in evil but rejoices
with the truth."[39]

"Honor your father and mother"…is the first
commandment with a promise *(Ephesians 6:2).*

~~~

Dennis Rainey, in *The Tribute: What Every Parent Longs to Hear,* wrote,

> Your children want more than anything else
> for you to be involved in their lives. They need
> more than your time—they need your atten-
> tion. They flourish when you focus on them.
> That means more than just showing up at
> soccer games with a cellular phone in your
> pocket. Your children need your heart knit-
> ted to theirs as they make their choices and
> hammer out their character. They need you to
> know what's going on in their lives…
>
> In order to be a parent worthy of honor you
> can't just "be there." As much as possible, you
> have to "be *all* there." That may sound simple,
> but it's easy for all your hours away from work
> to be filled with television shows, projects,
> finances, books, shopping, and housework. If
> you were able to add up how much time you
> actually spend focusing on your children each
> week, you might be shocked to discover your
> total measured in minutes, not hours…
>
> Being all there means that you are keep-
> ing the lines of communication firmly open
> and intact.[40]

Live…as wise, making the most of every
opportunity *(Ephesians 5:16).*

❧

The clock reminds us. Our stomach reminds us. Others remind us of this precious commodity called time. As a parent, you look at your child and think, *Where has the time gone? It seems like just yesterday she was starting school, and now she's graduating.* Sometimes we feel as if a thief came through the door and stole some of our time.

We all have a different value on time and its usage. Some people actually wonder what they can do to fill their time each day. They must not be parents! Sometimes you ask your children, "What have you been doing?" You hear the reply, "Just hanging around. You know, spending time bumming around." But time is more than something to be spent. When a portion of time in our life is gone, it can never be retrieved. It's gone forever.

One of the greatest gifts we can ever give another person is the gift of our time, whether it be to a family member, friend, or stranger.[41]

Moreover [let us also be full of joy now!] let us
exalt and triumph in our troubles and rejoice
in our sufferings, knowing that pressure and
affliction and hardship produce patient and
unswerving endurance *(Romans 5:3 AMP)*.

L osses. Your children will experience many of them.
Some daily. Part of your calling will be to assist them
to handle and learn from them. But before this can occur
we have to make sure we've handled the childhood losses
in our own life and recovered from them. Some adults
haven't.

Think about your life as a child. Have you identified
the losses? Do they loom out of proportion to all of your
experiences and affect the way you perceive all of your
life? Frequently this happens. We all perceive life from
our backlog of experiences.

In spite of this, there can be joy in the midst of difficulty. As you learn this, teach your children about life,
loss, and joy. It will prepare them for the future.

I urge you, brothers, by our Lord Jesus Christ and
by the love of the Spirit, to join me in my struggle
by praying to God for me *(Romans 15:30)*.

～⌘～

This is a blunt question: Do you pray regularly with
your partner? If you're a single parent, do you pray
regularly with a prayer partner or close friend?

One husband and father suggested that praying
together as a couple at bedtime does several things. It's
difficult to stay angry and distant from your spouse
when you pray with him or her. Second, when you pray
together, it seems that the Holy Spirit bonds your marriage together in a stronger way. Third, when you pray
together, it reminds you of what is important not only to
you but to your partner. Fourth, parenting is teamwork,
not just between a couple but with God.

Perhaps prayer is already a major part of your life
together. If not, why not begin now? It can only help and
may become a life-changing experience.[42]

Give thanks in all circumstances, for this is God's
will for you in Christ Jesus *(1 Thessalonians 5:18).*

❧

"P raise the Lord!" You've heard people say that. Perhaps you've said that too. It's easy to praise God for
what He has already done because we can reflect back
and measure the results. But what about praising Him
for what He is *going* to do? When you do that, you not
only become more of a risk taker, but you also become
aware of what He wants for you.

You will have circumstances in which there appears
to be no answer or solution. You may feel blocked. Have
you ever stopped at such times and taken a moment to
praise God? We are to recognize and rejoice in God. We
are to praise Him for who He is in response to His love,
goodness, faithfulness, and unbelievable concern for each
of us.

You may be thinking that you are too busy during
the day to stop and praise God. That, however, is just
the time to praise Him—when you are too busy, fret-
ful, and overwhelmed. You will feel refreshed when you
praise God!

God so loved the world that he gave his one
and only Son, that whoever believes in him shall
not perish but have eternal life *(John 3:16).*

✤

*F*amily. What does this word mean to you? What
images unfold in your mind as you focus on that
word? For many of us, family means the people we can
count on no matter what. Those special people who are
there when we need them. Those with whom we share
our joys and sorrows. Those who show up at our gradu-
ations, weddings, and when we're in the hospital. Family
usually includes the people you immediately look to for
help, support, love, and acceptance.

What does your family mean to you? Who has come
and gone? What marks have different people made on
your life? What imprints have you made—and are making—on others? Who are the people in your life you
consider family?

I urge you, brothers, in view of God's mercy, to offer
your bodies as living sacrifices *(Romans 12:1)*.

❧

How is your body today? Take a look at it in the mirror. How are the bodies of your family members? You've probably got all shapes and sizes in your household. It's interesting to note and understand what Scripture says about your body.

First, you don't own your body. It's not yours. It never was and never will be. Your children's bodies are not their own either. Our bodies belong to God. We are to present them to Him as sacrifices. But ours is a *living* sacrifice. We're a walking around and breathing sacrifice. People should be able to look at us and say, "There's a sacrifice to God." But would they end that comment with an exclamation point or a question mark? An exclamation point says, "You're in great shape! Wow!" A question mark says, "You're a living sacrifice? You've got to be kidding!"

So how are you treating your body? What shape are you in? Are you a living sacrifice?

Dear children, let us not love with words or tongue
but with actions and in truth *(1 John 3:18).*

～

"I love you." Three of the most commonly expressed words. Three of the most desired words to hear from loved ones. Parents and children exchange them, sometimes with deep feeling and thought. At other times, we say them automatically, as if we were giving a conditioned response. The words are easy to say, but difficult to do. If there are no actions to back them up, they have a hollow ring to them.

In today's verse God is saying, "If you say you love Me and other people, don't tell Me. Show Me. Be a person and family of action. Do something about the needs of other people. Then experience all the blessings I have for you."

That's quite an offer. In addition, God wouldn't ask us to do something we're incapable of doing. Are you ready to apply what you've learned? Make today interesting by reaching out to someone.

He who loves me will be loved by my Father, and I too will love him and show myself to him *(John 14:21)*.

Five of the most wonderful words that you can ever hear are "I will always love you." They are said by little children as they look up into the faces of their parents as they're being tucked into bed at the end of an exciting day. They are said by parents to their child as they close the door of their child's overloaded car before he or she departs for college. They are said with a look, a touch, a whisper, a note, or a shout.

These words are cherished by the person who receives them, for they bring inner peace and joy when all else has fallen apart. They are also noted by their absence, for there is an empty place in every person's heart that can only be filled by these five simple words. Without these words, we may question our worth.

There is one Person who never stops saying "I will always love you." Even when you don't hear it, it's being said. Even when you think you don't deserve it, it's being said. Are you listening?

Since we are surrounded by such a great cloud of
witnesses, let us throw off everything that hinders and
the sin that so easily entangles, and let us run with
perseverance the race marked out for us *(Hebrews 12:1)*.

Ｗe live in a world of gadgetry: airplanes, ships, and
missiles—and all have guidance-control systems.
That system is present for an important reason—to keep
the object on course so it will arrive at its destination. A
plane leaving Los Angeles for New York can end up hun-
dreds of miles off course with just the slightest variance
in directional readings.

For parents to be successful we need to stay on course,
know what we want to accomplish, let nothing distract us,
and persist in doing it. What do you want to accomplish?
What is your goal for your children? Is the goal yours...
or your partner's, your parents', your in-laws', or someone else's? Think about what you want, and consider how
it lines up with what God wants for you and your child.

Do not conform any longer to the pattern
of this world, but be transformed by the
renewing of your mind *(Romans 12:2)*.

How much have you changed recently? Perhaps change isn't uppermost in your mind because you feel you're doing all you can just to keep up with life as it is. And yet you are changing even though you may not realize it.

Well, at least I hope you and I are changing. The opposite of change (which means growing) is stagnation. We either change for the worse or the better. Your children are constantly changing too, as is your spouse.

Do you resist change or encourage it? Do you allow other people to encourage you to change? According to God's perspective, change is a crucial part of life. Have you considered how you would like your partner to change? Or how you would like your children to change? How will you be changing today? How do you think people in your family would like you to change? Why not get together and talk about change as a family?

You turned my wailing into dancing; you removed
my sackcloth and clothed me with joy, that my
heart may sing to you and not be silent. O LORD my
God, I will give you thanks forever *(Psalm 30:11-12)*.

⌘

What do you believe about life? How does your theology affect what you believe? When you encounter the difficulties and rough times in life, how do you reconcile everything? Did you know that our beliefs can create some of our tension? For example, some Christians live by assumptions that are not biblically based:

- Life is fair.
- I can control what happens to me.
- If I follow Christ and His teachings, nothing tragic will happen to me.
- If I am suffering, it is because I sinned or am sinning.
- My body was meant to live forever...at least until age 90.
- If I tithe, God will bless me financially.

It's important to make sure your beliefs are founded on the Word of God—especially before you hit rough times.

"Love the Lord your God with all your heart and with all your soul and with all your strength and with all your mind"; and "Love your neighbor as yourself" *(Luke 10:27)*.

M ost parents want their children to be loving individuals. They tell them this in many ways—sometimes in a soft, loving voice and other times in a loud, harsh manner. We all laugh at the frustrated parent who yells, "You're going to love your brother or I'll give you a spanking so you will remember!"

Talking about love isn't enough. Talk is cheap. Love must be *experienced,* especially by our children. What's the best way to teach them? By the three E's:

- *Example.* Our example shows our children what is possible.

- *Expectation.* When our children know we believe they're capable, they'll rise to the occasion.

- *Experience.* When our children see and feel love, they know it's real and can return it. God's love is the only power that can change people.

If your child ever says, "I can't love; it's too hard," don't buy it. Your child needs to know that when God asks us to do something, He equips us to do it.[43]

Do not store up for yourselves treasures on earth,
where moth and rust destroy, and where thieves
break in and steal. But store up for yourselves
treasures in heaven *(Matthew 6:19-20)*.

～⌇

One of the lessons of life that children (and parents) have to learn is how to put "first things first." Kids usually like to play before doing homework or practicing their music lessons. There are days when all of us look at the tasks to be done and feel like thumbing our noses at them. And sometimes we struggle with trying to decide what is most important. We have good intentions of what we're going to accomplish on Saturday, and then the distracting phone call or invitation comes in.

What we do and where we commit our time may need to be evaluated frequently. There are three great questions to ask: "Why am I doing what I'm doing?"; "For whose benefit or glory is this being done?"; and "What would life be like if I didn't do some of what I'm doing now?"[44]

Give thanks in all circumstances, for this is God's
will for you in Christ Jesus *(1 Thessalonians 5:18)*.

✎

"Thank you." "Thanks." "Thanks a lot." All these are phrases we begin teaching our children at an early age. We want them to be polite, appreciative, and thankful. But did you know there is another important reason for them—and us—to be thankful? Thankfulness is actually a prerequisite for worship. Scripture says, "Enter his gates with thanksgiving and his courts with praise; give thanks to him and praise his name" (Psalm 100:4).

Thankfulness is an attitude that needs to be developed. How? By becoming more aware of every good thing you have and experience in life. It's a refashioning of our attitude not to demand or expect something, but to experience everything—good and bad—as a gift. It means stopping, looking back over the last few hours, and saying, "I don't understand why I experienced that, but I am being blessed by God."[45]

Rejoice in the Lord always *(Philippians 4:4).*

❧

Do you ever want to resign from life? Especially on the days that Murphy's Law is in effect? Do you remember those laws? Here are some:

- Nothing is as easy as it looks.
- Everything takes longer than you think it will.
- If anything can go wrong, it will.

Have you ever...

- walked into the bathroom and stepped on a fur ball the cat left?
- changed the baby's diaper and tried to drop it into the diaper pail but it landed on your bare foot?
- had a child who bit into a strawberry and found an earwig in it?

The list of calamities could go on and on. (By the way, all these have happened to me!) At times like these, pray for patience—immediately.

In love he predestined us to be adopted as his sons
through Jesus Christ…to the praise of his glorious
grace, which he has freely given us *(Ephesians 1:5-6).*

There may be a thief living in your home—one that
steals joy and satisfaction. It could be residing in the
lives of one or more people in your family. It's called
perfectionism. Sure we all want to be successful, but perfectionism can become a mental monster.

Have you ever met perfectionists? They strive to do the
impossible and expect it from their children. The standards they set for themselves and their children…forget
it. No one could consistently attain them. Perfectionists
have a pet statement: "It could always be better." Things
are never good enough even when they are outstanding.
And this message is often conveyed to their children.

Keep in mind that perfectionism is not attainable nor
is it a spiritual calling. We are who we are because of what
God has done for us.

Though the LORD is on high, he looks upon the lowly,
but the proud he knows from afar *(Psalm 138:6).*

꙳

God is holy. There's an unapproachable holiness to
Him. But sometimes we have a wrong picture of
God because of the way we perceive His holiness. Our
Father is not a stern or harsh God. Consider what A.W.
Tozer says about Him:

> How good it would be if we could learn that
> God is easy to live with. He remembers our
> frame and knows that we are dust. He may
> sometimes chasten us, it is true, but even
> this he does with a smile, the proud tender
> smile of a Father who is bursting with plea-
> sure over an imperfect but promising son
> who is coming every day to look more and
> more like the One whose child he is.[46]

What a pattern and model for us in our response to
our family. Think about it: Do we burst with pleasure
when we see our partner, sons, and daughters? If so, do
they know it?

His delight is in the law of the LORD, and on his
law he meditates day and night *(Psalm 1:2)*.

A re you looking for surefire ways to help your children learn to live godly lives? There is a way that will develop character and help your children resist the pressures of negative life. The procedure is found in Psalm 1:2. You need to help them enjoy reading God's Word, contemplate what God's telling them, and put what they're learning into practice. The law is the Scripture, so if children want a clear, unwatered-down standard of right and wrong, they'll find it in the Word.

Do you know what the word *delight* means? Psalm 1:2 is saying that a godly person enjoys and wants the Word of God in his or her life. And meditation is not a nebulous, vague procedure. It means to place your mind on the Word, ponder it, think about it.

Why not commit Scripture verses to memory so they will come to mind when you need them?

The LORD is good and his love endures
forever; his faithfulness continues through
all generations *(Psalm 100:5)*.

᠉᠉

A couple stood at the doorway of their home watching their last child drive away to take a job across the country. As they closed the door, they turned and walked silently through the house. It was still filled with furniture, but there was an emptiness about it. They held hands without saying a word.

They knew they would be sad for a while. They had talked about this day, planned for it, and traveled the road that all parents will. You sink your very life into your children just to have them leave your nest. That's the way it is. It's hard, but it's good. If you haven't experienced it yet, you will. You're helping to build the future generation. Here's a great quote:

> Having children is a little like building ships. There comes a day when you have completed everything, and the ship needs to be launched.[47]

Before they call I will answer; while they are
still speaking I will hear *(Isaiah 65:24)*.

❧

Have you tried to call someone repeatedly only to get a busy signal? Perhaps you use the redial button, and the results are still the same...busy! Have you ever felt that way when it comes to praying...that the line is busy? Some people have. But God is not too busy. He always hears. He knows what you're going to say before you say it.

But there's another problem we sometimes encounter on the phone that can be even more frustrating. Have you ever received a phone call during which the other person talked on and on and on? The person would ask you a question, but before you could get your mouth open, he or she would answer it! You had something to say but the person hung up before you had a chance to do so. That's frustrating!

Prayers can be like that at times. We cut short some of our conversations with God or we don't listen. Can you relate?

I was shown mercy so that in me, the worst of
sinners, Christ Jesus might display his unlimited
patience as an example for those who would believe
on him and receive eternal life *(1 Timothy 1:16)*.

U nlimited patience. Wouldn't you like to have that?
It would be especially helpful with the children,
on the freeways, in the lines at supermarkets, and when
we're using the phone menus when we call a business
number.

Patience shows compassion for the frailties of others.
Jesus gives us many examples of when we need to be
patient with people. For instance, He was patient toward
forgetfulness. And we do forget. We want others to accept
our forgetfulness, but how do we respond when they
forget what we said?

One last thought: Could there be times when we've
forgotten the power of Jesus? Could there be times when
we've forgotten to say thanks? Sure, we've all done that.
But we have a Lord who has unlimited patience. He
knows we'll do better next time.[48]

I can do everything through him who
gives me strength *(Philippians 4:13)*.

~≫~

H ave you heard your children making statements
such as these? And are they a regular part of your
vocabulary?

- "I can't..."
- "That's a problem."
- "I'll never..."

Did you know that phrases like these reinforce the
control problems and hurts have over your life? Consider
what happens when you exchange these phrases for words
that better express your position in Christ.

- *"I can't."* It's no harder to say, "It's worth
  a try."
- *"That's a problem."* Using phrases such as
  "That's a challenge" or "That's an opportunity to learn something new" leaves the
  door open for moving ahead.
- *"I'll never..."* "I've never considered that
  before" or "I haven't done this before, but
  I'm willing to try" opens the door to personal growth.

Notice who in your family uses those negative phrases,
and encourage them to learn the alternatives.

I can do everything through him who
gives me strength *(Philippians 4:13)*.

～

"Why is life this way?" and its companion statement *"Life isn't fair"* are often overused for the normal, minor upsets of everyday life. Life is unpredictable and unfair. But our response to life is a choice, and the healthiest response is reflected in James 1:2-3: "Consider it wholly joyful, my brethren, whenever you are enveloped in or encounter trials of any sort, or fall into various temptations. Be assured and understand that the trial and proving of your faith bring out endurance and steadfastness and patience" (AMP). These verses encourage us to welcome or be glad about adversity.

Joy in life is a choice. And change in life can be a choice. *"If only..."* This phrase makes us "yesterday people" and imprisons us in lost dreams.

There is a phrase that can release us from yesterday and usher us into the future though. When we say *"Next time,"* we show that we have given up our regrets, learned from the past, and are getting on with our lives.

You are the salt of the earth. But if the salt loses
its saltiness, how can it be made salty again? It is
no longer good for anything, except to be thrown
out and trampled by men *(Matthew 5:13)*.

⇥

Have you ever eaten food that needed salt, but you
didn't have any? Or have you picked up food that
you thought hadn't been salted and dumped more on it so
that it was not edible? Notice that in Matthew 5:13 Jesus
didn't ask, "Do you want to be salt?" He wasn't making
a request. You are salt—clear and simple.

What does it mean to live as salt? Salt is distinctive. It
has its own task. It stands out. And if we're salt, we're to
do the same. One of the major qualities of salt in Jesus'
day was its ability to preserve. It was used to hold off
decay and keep food fresh.

Why not become a little more salty? Speak up with an
attitude of love. The best way to be salt is to bring others
to a saving knowledge of Jesus Christ.[49]

Why spend money on what is not bread, and
your labor on what does not satisfy? Listen, listen
to me, and eat what is good, and your soul will
delight in the richest of fare *(Isaiah 55:2).*

Y ou're at the doctor's office for your annual physical.
You've reached the age where it's necessary to take a
treadmill stress test for your heart. You go into the room,
get wired up, and once the treadmill is running, you step
on. You walk...and keep walking. You pass the 10-minute
mark, and your heart is pounding. Finally it's over. You
walked rapidly for 12 minutes and got...nowhere. You
got on and off in the same location.

Do you ever feel that life is one big treadmill? Always
going and never getting anywhere? If so, it could be
because often we just respond to what happens around
us rather than creatively orchestrating our future. Or it
could be because our priorities are not God's priorities.

Before you make a decision about what to do, ask
God for His opinion.

Since we are surrounded by such a great cloud of
witnesses, let us throw off everything that hinders and
the sin that so easily entangles, and let us run with
perseverance the race marked out for us *(Hebrews 12:1)*.

~≫≪~

Runners are a different kind of people. Jeanne Zornes reminds us of four things as we run this race called life.

- *Remember you're watched.* We're actually on display in our Christian life.

- *When you run, run light.* When runners prepare for a race they leave nothing to chance. They strip off every possible ounce. Likewise we're to strip off everything that keeps us from doing our best such as anger, lack of control, procrastination, eating habits that aren't healthy, overloaded schedules, addictions...

- *Never give up.* Don't quit. Persevere and continue to trust God to bring that finish line into view.

- *Keep your focus.* You're not running for you but for God. Fix your eyes on Jesus—when you do, you draw strength from Him to finish the race and to cope with the children.[50]

O LORD, you have searched me and you know
me. You know when I sit and when I rise; you
perceive my thoughts from afar *(Psalm 139:1-2)*.

*P*atience. A commodity most of us want…right now.
We need it as we deal with our children, our spouses,
and even ourselves. Some of us are impatient with our
own progress—or lack of it—as we struggle to be different in some way. But you can change…and you will
change. And so will your children.

Yet transformation takes time. It's slow. Scripture
promises that even something as difficult as our thought
lives (from which comes our feelings, actions, and words)
can change. Second Corinthians 10:5 says to "take captive
every thought to make it obedient to Christ." Romans
12:2 says, "Do not conform any longer to the pattern of
this world, but be transformed by the renewing of your
mind."

If you struggle with your thoughts, turn back to the
Scriptures and ask God's intervention to help your mind
become new. He wouldn't have said these things if they
couldn't happen.

I have fought the good fight, I have finished the
race, I have kept the faith. Now there is in store for
me the crown of righteousness *(2 Timothy 4:7)*.

‿✦‿

As believers, we will someday receive four different and
wonderful crowns. One is the *Crown of Righteousness,* which is mentioned in today's verse. This crown is
for believers who look forward to the return of Jesus.

Then there is the *Crown of Life,* which is for those
who allow the love of God to permeate and sustain them
(James 1:12).

Third, there is a *Crown of Rejoicing.* For Paul it was
comprised of the people he had brought to Jesus. There
is no greater joy than leading another person to the Lord
(1 Thessalonians 2:9).

Finally, there is the *Crown of Glory* (1 Peter 5:4).

There is one other crown we need to remember. It was
Jesus' crown—*a crown of thorns* that He wore for you and
me and the entire world. His crown enables us to someday wear a crown.[51]

In my Father's house are many rooms; if it
were not so, I would have told you. I am going
there to prepare a place for you *(John 14:2)*.

———

Y ou may have heard people who are elderly or termi-
nally ill say, "I'm just waiting around for heaven." How
many of us in the prime of life have a longing for heaven?
Not many. Perhaps this is because we don't know or understand what it will be like.

> We may think we're waiting for heaven. *But
> heaven is waiting for us.* God is not, as many
> say, getting our mansions ready. *He's get-
> ting us ready for our mansions.*[52]

Will you feel comfortable in the presence of Jesus?
When you're standing in front of Him, looking Him in
the face, what will He be like? That's difficult to compre-
hend, but John says we'll be like Him (1 John 3:2), so in
our new and changed state we ought to feel comfortable in
His presence. Once we become Christians, every moment
of our lives goes toward getting ready for heaven.[53]

These are the commands…the LORD your God directed
me to teach you…so that you, your children and their
children after them may fear the LORD *(Deuteronomy 6:2)*.

A family is made up of more than you and your children. You have a heritage. You have your parents, and they had theirs. Each generation has something to pass on to the next. What can you pass on to your children from the lives of those who came before you? How much do your parents know of their grandparents, great-grandparents, and so on? Each family member, past and present, is part of the collage that makes up your larger family. And there's a purpose in the life of each member. As Edith Schaeffer says,

> A family—parents and grandparents and children, the larger combination of three or four generations, or one little two-generation family—is meant to be a picture of what God is to His Family.[54]

Those who know your name will trust in
you, for you, LORD, have never forsaken
those who seek you *(Psalm 9:10)*.

Special Thoughts for Mothers

Ruth Bell Graham said, "As a mother, my job is to take care of the possible and trust God with the impossible."

Henry Ward Beecher said, "A mother has, perhaps, the hardest earthly lot; and yet no mother worthy of the name ever gave herself thoroughly for her child who did not feel that, after all, she reaped what she had sown."

Glen Wheeler adds, "Through the ages no nation has had a better friend than the mother who taught her child to pray."

Helen Steiner Rice noted, "A mother's love is patient and forgiving when all others are forsaking, and it never fails or falters, even though the heart is breaking."

James Keller said, "Every mother has the breathtaking privilege of sharing with God in the creation of new life. She helps bring into existence a soul that will endure for all eternity."

An anonymous writer penned, "A mother is the one who is still there when everyone else has deserted you."

The prayer of a righteous man is powerful
and effective *(James 5:16)*.

⇥

Some parents read books about parenting. That's good. Some parents make sure their children go to church, read their Bible, and attend Christian schools. That's good too. Some parents are intercessors for their children through faithful prayer. That's even better!

If you want to see an example of a parent who prayed for his children, look at Job. In the first chapter you discover that after Job's children feasted, Job would have them purified. "Early in the morning he would sacrifice a burnt offering for each of them, thinking, 'Perhaps my children have sinned and cursed God in their hearts'" (Job 1:5). He was concerned and faithful in bringing them before the Lord.

John Bunyan made an interesting comment about prayer many years ago. He said,

> You can do more than pray
> after you have prayed
> But you cannot do more than pray
> until you have prayed.

How are you praying for your children? And have you asked them to pray for you?

You have taken off your old self...and have put on
the new self, which is being renewed in knowledge
in the image of its Creator *(Colossians 3:9-10)*.

H ave you ever thought about yourself as a work of art?
You are. So is each child. Consider this: "When a
fanatic dealt several damaging blows to Michelangelo's
Pieta, the world was horrified. It surprised no one when
the world's best artists assembled to refashion the disfigured masterpiece."[55] Sometimes we disfigure ourselves
by what we think about ourselves rather than what we
do to ourselves. Some people have been disfigured emotionally because of what others did to them when they
were children.

In a sense, you are a sculptor fashioning your children. The words and looks you use are the tools that leave
imprints. And you too are a work of art. You're a masterpiece! God's art created in Jesus Christ. And you're more
valuable to Him than any museum piece. What do you
think about that?

Let us not lose heart in doing good, for in due time we will reap if we do not grow weary *(Galatians 6:9 NASB)*.

⌇

I n *Wait Quietly: Devotions for Busy Parents,* Dean Merrill shares this advice:

> When you're switching Laundry Load No. 6 into the dryer and there are two loads yet to wash...when you write the check for your child's music lessons and *again* there's nothing left for an adult night out...when you play an after-supper game with your kids, then read them a bedtime story, pray with them, and finally tuck them in, only to realize you're too tired to tackle that job you'd saved for this evening...you need the apostle's exhortation in [Galatians 6:9]...
>
> Parenting is like farming: a lot of hard work, day in and day out, month in and month out, and the "harvest of blessing" doesn't come quickly...*Having* kids is the easy part: a nine-month incubation that climaxes in the thrill of a new arrival. *Raising* kids, by comparison, takes twenty-five times as long and probably a hundred times as much endurance and fortitude.[56]

Honor your father and your mother *(Exodus 20:12)*.

～⫸～

How old are you today? How many more years will it be until you're 65? 75? 80? Kind of scary, isn't it? Have you ever tried to imagine what you will be like at 80 years of age? It's ironic—we start out in life dependent on others, and in some ways end up like that. We start out being parented. Later we get married, become parents, and then…we may end up being parented again. Only this time by our children.

How will your children respond to you when you're old? How will they treat and parent you? There are two possibilities: Either they will treat you the way they were parented or the way they observed you parenting your parents. That makes you stop and think, doesn't it? You're not only raising your children to be functional, responsible, independent adults, you're also raising them to take care of you when you're elderly.

What do your children hear and observe from you about the way you relate to your parents?

"Come, follow me," Jesus said, "and I will
make you fishers of men" *(Matthew 4:19)*.

⁓

I have absolute confidence in you. I believe you have
the ability and the wisdom to do what I'm asking you
to do. Go for it!" Great words of encouragement, aren't
they? That's what Jesus is saying to every believer in Mark
4:19. He is saying, "Tell other people about Me. You can
do it!"

Many Christians hesitate, however. It's a bit scary to
tell other people about Him. But God will give us the
words when we need them. You don't have to struggle to
assemble a collection of pat phrases ahead of time. Ask
Him for opportunities as well as the words, and believe
He will give them to you.

Jesus doesn't want you to be silent about Him. He
empowers you to share and then proclaims that you are
His. He has confidence in you. Doesn't that make it a
lot easier for you to share your faith?[57]

Be strong in the grace that is in
Christ Jesus *(2 Timothy 2:1)*.

❧

The Scripture gives us a model for parenting that is based on our relationship with God. If you read through the book of Psalms, you can discover some of the roles a father has in relation to his children—roles that are based on how God responds to us:

> The LORD is my light and my salvation—whom shall I fear? The LORD is the stronghold of my life—of whom shall I be afraid? (Psalm 27:1).

> The LORD is gracious and compassionate, slow to anger and rich in love (Psalm 145:8).

As parents, we will be called upon many times to be our children's source of security and a refuge who is approachable and supportive. But to be able to do this consistently we will need to rely on our heavenly Father in the same way to have our own needs filled. Yes, our children will depend upon us, but it's so much easier when, at the same time, we're dependent on God.

Woe to you, teachers of the law and Pharisees,
you hypocrites! *(Matthew 23:25).*

～⌒～

The Pharisees were image-conscious. They worked at
looking a certain way to make an impression on others.
They really weren't all that different from us today. Instead
of working on developing inner character qualities, we
concern ourselves with polishing our image.

We also want our children to behave perfectly when
we're with company and at certain functions. Why? We
want our homes to look impeccable when guests come
over. Why? In many ways we are like that little lizard
that children like to have as a pet—the chameleon. We
change colors frequently. We don't change colors to avoid
danger (as the lizard does), but to gain approval.

So how do we stop being hypocritical? First, remind
yourself that you don't need the approval of others. Let
God work on changing you on the inside. When that's
done, you'll feel more secure and the necessary outward
changes will begin to take place. Your true colors will
show. After all, who wants to be a lizard?[58]

Christ the power of God and the wisdom
of God *(1 Corinthians 1:24)*.

❦

Power failure. The lights dim, then go out. The sounds of machinery—the refrigerator or air conditioners—come to a halt. Usually it happens when the people who are tapping into the power source overload it. Or it could be there is a short in the system or a transformer wore out.

Here are a couple of questions. First, who is your power source? Is it you? Your spouse? Your friends? The Lord? Some of us go through life connected to a real power source, and others run their lives on a portable battery pack powered by their own energy. And naturally they run out of juice after a while. But when your source is the Lord, there's never any lack of potential power.

The next question is, Are you plugged in? An electric saw won't work when you run the blade back and forth by hand. It's got to be connected. Plug into Jesus. He's the ultimate power source.[59]

You shall teach [my words] diligently to your sons
and shall talk of them when you sit in your house
and when you walk by the way and when you lie
down and when you rise up *(Deuteronomy 6:7 NASB)*.

A young man was asked where he learned most of his
values. "Well, it really wasn't in school. It wasn't in
books or from sermons. It was my mom and dad." Dr.
Charles Swindoll says that the family is...

> The relay place. A race with a hundred
> batons...
>
> - *Honesty.* "Speak and live the truth—
>   always."
>
> - *Responsibility.* "Be dependable, be trust-
>   worthy."
>
> - *Thoughtfulness.* "Think of others before
>   yourself."
>
> - *Confidentiality.* "Don't tell secrets. Seal
>   your lips."...
>
> - *Patience.* "Fight irritability. Be willing
>   to wait."
>
> - *Purity.* "Reject anything that lowers your
>   standards."[60]

Cast all your anxiety on him because
he cares for you *(1 Peter 5:7)*.

～❦～

W hat does a "good enough" parent look like? The best
model is the way God parents us. Myron Chartier
describes some of His attributes:

- *God cares for people* (see Luke 15:11-32;
  1 Peter 5:7).

- *God is responsive to human needs.* We see this
  in God's freely given grace, mercy, and restoration (see John 3:16; Titus 3:3-7).

- *God reveals love by giving.* He gave us His
  only Son and the power to become His children (John 3:16; 3:1-2).

- *God shows respect.* He values and cherishes
  us and let's us be free to be rather than
  being dominated or possessed.

- *God knows us.* His Son was made in human
  likeness (see John 1:14; Philippians 2:5-8;
  Hebrews 2:17-18; 4:15).

- *God forgives us* (see Ephesians 1:7; John 3:17;
  Hebrews 4:15-16).[61]

I have been crucified with Christ and I no longer
live, but Christ lives in me. The life I live in the
body, I live by faith in the Son of God, who loved
me and gave himself for me *(Galatians 2:20)*.

~≈~

There's no doubt about it. Paul was a committed apostle. He was committed to Jesus, and he committed his difficulties to Him as well. In today's verse, the Greek word for "committed" refers to a deposit given to another person for safekeeping. What's involved in a person's commitment to the Lord? Dr. Lloyd John Ogilvie suggests three elements:

- The first is *repentance*. This means returning to the Lord and changing our belief that we're on our own and that we have to face life in our own strength.

- The second is *relinquishment* of our struggles and facing what is driving us up the wall.

- The third part of commitment is *responsiveness*. It's asking several times a day, "I wonder what the Lord has in store for me with this?" and then doing what He asks.[62]

The tongue of the wise commends knowledge, but
the mouth of the fool gushes folly *(Proverbs 15:2)*.

❧

The book of Proverbs is a wonderful and practical book
for families to live by—especially in what they say
to one another. Our mouths can be used in healthy or
unhealthy ways. Let's consider what Proverbs says about
an uncontrolled tongue.

Deceitful flattery. "Food gained by fraud tastes
sweet to a man, but he ends up with a mouth
full of gravel" (Proverbs 20:17).

Gossip and slander. "He who conceals his hatred
has lying lips, and whoever spreads slander is
a fool" (10:18).

Angry words. "An angry man stirs up dissension,
and a hot-tempered one commits many sins"
(29:22).

Boasting. "Like clouds and wind without rain is
a man who boasts of gifts he does not give"
(25:14).

Talking too much. "When words are many, sin is
not absent, but he who holds his tongue is wise"
(10:19). When we talk, we aren't listening. It's
only when we listen that we learn.

Are any of these familiar?

We all stumble in many ways. If anyone is never
at fault in what he says, he is a perfect man, able
to keep his whole body in check *(James 3:2)*.

~

Control. It's highly desired, frequently absent, and sometimes overused. But when it comes to controlling our mouths, it is essential. A mouth out of control is like a runaway train ready to jump the track and create havoc all around it. If you want some guidance on positive ways of speaking to your children (and others!), look to the book of Proverbs.

- First, parents (and all of us) are to give wise counsel and sound advice (10:32).

- Parents are called upon to give reproof, rebuke, and especially spiritual exhortation (15:5,31-32).

- Parents are also asked to witness, teach, and comfort as well (25:11).

Did you know that the Word of God also asks you to have a sense of humor? "A cheerful look brings joy to the heart" (Proverbs 15:30). Humor is a lifesaver!

Because he himself suffered when he
was tempted, he is able to help those who
are being tempted *(Hebrews 2:18)*.

Satan is subtle. He attacks us in numerous ways, laying out temptations in front of us like stones on a path, hoping we'll trip over them. He tried to tempt Jesus too. But He countered Satan by saying, "You shall not tempt...the Lord your God" (Matthew 4:7; Deuteronomy 6:16). Satan offered Jesus the kingdoms of the world if He would worship him. Again Jesus confronted Satan with Scripture.

Notice that Jesus gave us an interesting strategy we can use when we are tempted. We can cite Scripture to kick Satan out of our lives.

How does Satan try to get through to you? Have you been pressured by other people to give in to what they want or believe? We conform because we don't want to be different. Yet it's okay to be different—to take an unpopular stand, to follow Jesus' leading. Think about that the next time you feel pressured.[63]

Bless the LORD, O my soul *(Psalm 103:1 NASB).*

〜

What does it mean to bless someone? To bless generally means to speak good or to do good for another person. There are many types of blessing in Scripture. One is the blessing *God communicates to people,* such as when he blessed Abraham: "I will make you into a great nation and I will bless you; I will make your name great, and you will be a blessing" (Genesis 12:2).

A second type of blessing is *spoken by people to God.* We honor God when we acknowledge Him as the source of all we have. (See Psalm 103:1-2.)

Yet another type is a blessing *spoken by God or people over things,* such as in Deuteronomy 28:4-5: "The fruit of your womb will be blessed, and the crops of your land…"

The fourth type of blessing is *spoken by one person to another,* often invoking the name of God, such as when Jacob blessed Pharaoh as a sign of respect or honor (see Genesis 47:7).[64]

Sometimes it's easier for us to give a verbal blessing than *to be a blessing* to someone.

> I became greater by far than anyone in Jerusalem
> before me...I hated life, because the work that is
> done under the sun was grievous to me. All of it is
> meaningless, a chasing after the wind *(Ecclesiastes 2:9,17)*.

Talk about extremes! One minute the writer of Ecclesiastes seems to be applauding himself, and the next he's in despair and regretting all that he has done. He is looking back after a life of effort and achievement and saying that he feels empty. "It wasn't worth it," he says. What a feeling of futility! He says,

> I hated all the things I had toiled for under
> the sun, because I must leave them to the
> one who comes after me. And who knows
> whether he will be a wise man or a fool?
> (verse 18).

Project yourself down the road a bit—to the end of your life. What do you want to be able to say about your life? You can determine that by what you do now.

Love bears up under anything and everything
that comes, is ever ready to believe the best
of every person *(1 Corinthians 13:7 AMP).*

～≠～

What can parents do to help their children accept who they are?

- Ask God to help you be aware of how you feel about yourself. Many parents are hard on their children because of their own unresolved issues.

- Ask God to help you appreciate the uniqueness of each one of your children and to be aware of their real needs.

- On a daily basis, tell your children you love them. Nothing defends against the attacks of shame or unworthiness like the security a child receives from the love and acceptance of his or her parents.

- Affirm your children several times a day. Let them know they are of infinite worth and value and are precious to you.

- Give them quality time.

- Listen for your kids' statements of guilt and shame.[65]

By the way, do you treat yourself in this way? It's a good place to begin.

In all your ways acknowledge him, and he will
make your paths straight *(Proverbs 3:6)*.

～

D o you ever catch yourself looking at the clock and
wondering, *Will I make it? Is there enough time to
get everything done?* Rush, rush, rush—that's the story
of our lives. We're on the go all the time at a rapid pace.
Who piles on the work? God? No. We do.

We need to pace ourselves. In races—whether horse,
auto, or human—there is often one who sets the pace.
What we need is a pacesetter. This rendition of a portion of
Psalm 23 by Toki Miyashina can help your perspective:

> The Lord is my Pacesetter, I shall
>   not rush;
> He makes me stop and rest for quiet
>   intervals.
> He provides me with images of
>   stillness, which restore my serenity;
> He leads me in the ways of efficiency
>   through calmness of mind,
> And His guidance is peace.
> Even though I have a great many
>   things to accomplish each day,
> I will not fret, for His presence is here.[66]

[The mystery] is now disclosed…Christ in
you, the hope of glory *(Colossians 1:26-27)*.

꧁꧂

H ave you ever felt like a ball of yarn with the threads
starting to come unraveled…and there's no way to
stop it? That's the way life is sometimes—slowly unrav-
eling. We have a phrase for that: "I feel like I'm at loose
ends!"

We all want to have complete control over our lives,
but we can't. God never intended for us to be in control.
Does that thought stress you or relax you? What happens
when we try to take control of our lives? Does it work?
No. Do we tend to mess up? Yes. God knows that, so He
gave that task to Jesus. There's just one catch. (Isn't there
usually?) We need to surrender our will to Him and admit
we can't control our lives. We also need to surrender to
Him our desire to be in control.

We make a choice about who should run our lives—
us or Him.[67]

Encourage (admonish, exhort) one another and
edify (strengthen and build up) one another, just
as you are doing *(1 Thessalonians 5:11 AMP)*.

❧

"Y ou can't change another person, so forget it." Have
you ever heard that statement? It's not necessarily true.
If you're a parent, you're called to be a change agent with
your children.

Another word for *change* is *grow*. You certainly would
like your children to grow. Some people object to the
idea of trying to change others, yet the Bible calls us to
help other people grow or change (see Acts 18:27; 1 Thessalonians 4:10).

What are we to exhort, teach, or encourage one another
to do? Love and help and comfort (1 Thessalonians 4:10;
Acts 18:27). Perhaps the ideas of exhorting and encouraging are new for you. Consider how you might incorporate
these principles when you raise your children and interact with your partner. But remember: Any change you
request in other people needs to be for their benefit. Present your requests thoughtfully and prayerfully.

After Paul had seen the vision, we got ready at once
to leave for Macedonia, concluding that God had
called us to preach the gospel to them *(Acts 16:10)*.

A s parents, we want to know the will of God for our
lives as well as for our families. How can we know?
If we have the inclination to know His will, if we have
looked into His Word, then we need to see…

> What [the Lord] wants us to do to cooperate
> with Him in the accomplishment of His will.
> The infilling of the Spirit creates the impulse,
> the inspiration, and the insight we need. The
> indwelling Lord creates the desire to do His
> will, convinces us of our new life in Him, and
> clarifies what we are to do in specific circum-
> stances.
>
> There are also three precious keys to the
> secret of guidance: commitment of our will,
> freedom from dependence on contemporary
> values which are not rooted in Christ, and
> bringing our outward life into conformity
> with the indwelling Christ through moment-
> by-moment renewal of our relationship with
> Him.[68]

Do not worry about tomorrow, for tomorrow
will worry about itself. Each day has enough
trouble of its own *(Matthew 6:34)*.

⌇⌇

When young men and women interview for a prospective job, they usually ask, "What are the retirement
benefits? What kind of pension do you have?" Sometimes
they will refuse job offers because of what *isn't* offered 40
or 50 years down the line. In other areas of life, we often
fall into the pattern of worrying about the future and fail
to enjoy today. We allow what may or may not happen
years from now to rob us of our joy at the present time.

> We drag tomorrow's imagined difficulties
>   into this day.
> So we desecrate each day with stress and
>   strain.
>   Our Father never intended us to live that
>   way.
> He gives us life one day at a time.
>   Yesterday is gone.
>   Only today is mine to relish at a
>   gentle pace.
> It is too precious to overload.
>   So it is to be enjoyed in serenity and strength.
>   Put first things first.
>   The petty distractions can wait.[69]

I know your deeds. See, I have placed before you
an open door that no one can shut. I know that
you have little strength, yet you have kept my word
and have not denied my name *(Revelation 3:8)*.

Most of us have been told to look for the "open doors of opportunity." Open doors are much easier to get through than closed doors. Jesus said to the church at Philadelphia, "I have placed before you an open door" (Revelation 3:8). He wants us to walk through the open doors of life, to try the untried, to be willing to be different, and to confront challenges that will push us to grow.

The open doorway that is beckoning to you is providing you with a unique opportunity to love others, to care in a new way, to do something that will make a difference. No one is going to shut the door from the outside. It stays open. Don't be immobilized. Walk through that doorway and discover what God has for you.

The love of money is a root of all
kinds of evil *(1 Timothy 6:10)*.

～

We all need money. Prices climb and the paycheck shrinks. The battle gets especially rough as our children grow up. Some people have a different problem with money—they love it. It becomes the reason for their existence, their goal in life. It's their god. What part does money play in your life? Think about these questions:

- What percentage of the day do you spend worrying about money?

- Do you spend more time thinking or worrying about money than you spend praying each day?

- Does the value you attach to yourself as a person fluctuate in accord with the fluctuation of your net worth?

- To what extent is money the source of arguments between you and other family members?

- To what extent do you and your family members pray about money and the direction God wants you to take in using it for His kingdom and glory?

Why not discuss these questions with your partner and family?[70]

Do not be anxious about anything, but in
everything, by prayer and petition, with thanksgiving,
present your requests to God *(Philippians 4:6).*

❧

As a parent, one of the struggles you face is ministering
to your children when they are sick. This prayer
by William Barclay from his *Book of Everyday Prayer,*
may be useful.

O God, our Father,
bless and help (name)
in the illness which has come upon
    him (her)…
Help us not to worry too much,
but to leave our loved one
in the hands of wise and skillful men
    (and women)
who have the gift of healing,
and in your hands.
Lord Jesus,
come to us and to our loved one…
and show us that your healing touch
has never lost its ancient power.
This we ask for thy love's sake. Amen.

When he saw the crowds, he went up on a
mountainside and sat down. His disciples came
to him, and he began to teach *(Matthew 5:1-2)*.

❦

What would it have been like to sit on a mountainside
and listen to Jesus teach? Probably uncomfortable.
Why? Well, the ground was hard and the rocks rough,
jagged, and unmoving. In addition, Jesus' teaching was
calling the people of His time—as well as ours—to a
new way of living.

The Sermon on the Mount is profound, practical, and
life-changing. It is a call to be different in every area of
life, including the way you parent. There are four ways
in which this difference is expressed.

- Your *morality* will be different.

- Your *mentality* will be different. Jesus' teachings came from heaven, so what you teach
  your children will be contrary to what the
  world teaches.

- *Mastery* is third. You are not in charge of
  your life.[71]

- You are going to be in the *minority*. Your
  morality, mentality, and mastery will set
  you apart from most of the world.

Think about that…today. Then act.

Wait for the LORD; be strong and take heart
and wait for the LORD *(Psalm 27:14)*.

✢

Much of our lives is spent waiting. There are waiting rooms in hospitals, airports, and train stations. People often say, "Why don't you sit down over there and wait?" Do you ever get the feeling that much of life is one big waiting room? We spend so much time waiting for our children to finish playing, get ready for school, get out of the bathroom, and come to dinner. It's aggravating to spend hours preparing a meal and then have to wait for the rest of the family while the food gets lukewarm.

Is there a purpose or benefit in waiting? Yes. It makes us realize how much we need God. It makes us more willing to receive Him. And it makes us able to handle what life throws our way. "Those who hope in the LORD will renew their strength. They will soar on wings like eagles; they will run and not grow weary, they will walk and not be faint" (Isaiah 40:31).

Waiting brings great rewards.

Praise be to the God and Father of our Lord Jesus
Christ, the Father of compassion and the God of all
comfort, who comforts us in all our troubles, so that we
can comfort those in any trouble with the comfort we
ourselves have received from God *(2 Corinthians 1:3-4)*.

When we travel through a time of loss, we are eager
for our grief to end. But grief doesn't have to be
a thief in the night that comes to steal away your joy. It
can be just the opposite: It can help us experience joy
once again. Grief is normal, necessary, and inevitable.
You, your spouse, and your children will experience losses
together and separately.

When a loved one enters into the valley of grief, they
need someone—namely you. Offering comfort is sitting
in silence while your child or spouse cries until it seems
his or her heart will break. It is sitting with your arms
around him or her and listening—no matter whether
what is said makes sense or not.

A record of the genealogy of Jesus Christ
the Son of David *(Matthew 1:1).*

A family tree is the history of how you came to be. For many people, keeping track of all the relatives and researching family roots has become quite a pastime. And it is a worthwhile venture to pass on to your children. One day you too will be an ancestor on that family tree!

Jesus was from the house of David. That may not mean much to you today, but had you lived in Jesus' day, that information was vital. Every Jewish person knew the Messiah had to come from the house or lineage of David.

Jesus' title as the Son of David brings in His connection with humanity. On the one hand He was God. But He was also man. He had two parents like everyone else. He is the Son of God and the Son of David. Have you introduced the living members of your past and present family tree to Jesus' family tree? How much do they know about Him?[72]

Let us stop passing judgment on one another. Instead,
make up your mind not to put any stumbling block
or obstacle in your brother's way *(Romans 14:13)*.

I f you've ever grown any plants, you know they often require as much care as children. One of the problems plants can have is to be hit by some sort of blight. *Webster's New World Dictionary* says a blight is any kind of an atmospheric or soil condition, parasite, or insect that kills or retards the growth of plants.

One of the blights that will destroy a relationship or friendship quicker than anything else is gossip. Some people use gossip as a cover for criticism. But the biggest danger of gossip is that it's usually not accurate. Even family members gossip about other family members.

How can you overcome gossiping or hinder its growth? It's simple. *Pray* for the person, check out any rumor to see if it's true and let the teller know when it's not, and don't repeat anything about another person you haven't said or aren't willing to say to that person within 24 hours. Will this make a major difference in the way you talk?[73]

These commandments that I give you today
are to be upon your hearts. Impress them
on your children *(Deuteronomy 6:6-7).*

~~

Many fathers do a wonderful job of raising their children. Too often people focus more on what they haven't done rather than what they've done right. We can learn the most from those examples that are positive. Here are some statements sons have said about their dads:

- "My father showed his feelings in actions, but most importantly, he verbalized them too."

- "He didn't blame us for the way he felt. I've also seen him grieve."

- "Dad expressed delight by the expression on his face, sorrow by withdrawing, frustrations by being busy and involved, but love by telling me, 'You're special, son. I love you. God blessed me when you came along.'"

What would you like your children to say about you when they reach adulthood? What happens now in your relationship with your sons and daughters will affect what they say about you in the future.

From the ends of the earth I call to you, I call as my
heart grows faint; lead me to the rock that is higher
than I...I long to dwell in your tent forever and take
refuge in the shelter of your wings *(Psalm 61:2,4).*

＊

"Don't cling to me. I can't stand it. You're old enough
to stand on your own." Those words are spoken in
frustration by many parents at one time or another. Children will cling, especially when they're learning to walk
or they're frightened. There are times when we encourage clinging. We tell children to "hang on" because we
know there are times when we all hang on to something
in an effort to survive.

And it's not just physical stress we battle. Mental or
emotional stress can upset us as well. That's when we
need something solid and secure to cling to so we can
make it through. Hang on tight to God and His Word.
Hang on as He wraps His arms around you. He can't
and won't be uprooted.

The LORD will be your confidence and will keep
your foot from being snared *(Proverbs 3:26).*

❧

*N*o. It's a simple two-letter word which, interestingly
enough, is one of the first words children learn to
say. And we quickly tire of hearing it. Yet it's a powerful
little word and a necessary one.

In the musical play *Oklahoma!* there's a song titled
"I'm Just a Girl Who Can't Say No." Is it difficult for you
to say no? Sometimes we're either afraid of the reaction
we'll get if we say no or we fear offending the person
who made the request. And yet some people are noted
for saying no immediately.

God wants us to say no—not to Him, but to many
other situations in life. Temptations swirl around us every
day just looking for a place to land. How can we be consistent in saying no when we need to? Just ask, "Will
saying yes bring me closer to the Lord?"

Do not fear, for I am with you *(Isaiah 41:10)*.

～

F ear is part of life, and it keeps us from getting the most out of life. Fear can talk us into limiting our vision, and as a result we do less than we're capable of doing. Fear can also cause us to imagine the worst possible outcome of our efforts. There are many things to fear as parents, so we may inadvertently limit the positive experiences available to our children. We focus on what *could* happen to them and imagine the worst.

Fear has a warping effect. It warps our perceptions of life and what we could do to move ahead in a positive way.[74] Fear keeps us from saying...

- I can
- I will
- I'm able
- God will help me do it
- God will take care of this

Conquer your own fears, and when your children ask you how to handle fear in their own lives, you'll have suggestions and encouragement you can give to them.

Do not be anxious about anything, but in
everything, by prayer and petition, with thanksgiving,
present your requests to God *(Philippians 4:6).*

※

Once again it's time to face the inevitable. One day
they'll be gone. No, not your hair or your teeth…
your kids. They'll walk out your front door and become
the next generation. It's normal to wonder what that experience will be like, how your kids will do, and how you'll
cope. Perhaps this mother's prayer voices what you may
struggle with. What do you think?

> Lord, as I face an empty nest, I am afraid.
> I'm afraid for Jason's safety…I'm afraid the
> house will be so empty without the noise
> of a teenager's laughter and the reverbera-
> tion of his karate practice…Teach me that
> "letting go" involves a total surrender of my
> will and a faith-filled decision to practice
> what Mary said: "Be it unto me according
> to Thy will." Help me to affirm my son's
> manhood and trust his choices. Teach me
> to "be anxious for nothing" and to quit
> worrying about tomorrow.[75]

I, the Teacher, was king over Israel in Jerusalem. I
devoted myself to study and to explore by wisdom
all that is done under heaven *(Ecclesiastes 1:12-13).*

⌇

Think back a few years to when you were a child. (Perhaps that's more than a few years.) Do you remember
what children think about constantly? What they have
on their minds while they're awake? What they want to
do most? Play!

Playing was one of the ways we prepared for the adult
world. We emulated what we saw and put our daydreams
into action. Our play may even have influenced what we
chose to do for our livelihoods.

Hopefully, you play often with your children. And
what about your own play? What do you do that you
thoroughly enjoy, that rejuvenates you, that brings a sense
of joy and lifts your outlook and approach to the tasks
of life? Everyone needs a break. If you don't take one,
you not only become too serious, but you'll also stagnate and wear out.

There is a time for everything, and a season for
every activity under heaven *(Ecclesiastes 3:1).*

❧

We talked about rhythm and balance earlier in this
devotional, but let's talk about them again. We
learned earlier that the four ingredients needed for healthy
balance are work, worship, rest, and play. It's easy to get
them mixed up.

Consider what Scripture has to say about the importance of rhythm and balance in life:

> As long as the earth endures, seedtime and har-
> vest, cold and heat, summer and winter, day
> and night will never cease (Genesis 8:22).

> I have seen something else under the sun:
> The race is not to the swift or the battle to
> the strong, nor does food come to the wise or
> wealth to the brilliant or favor to the learned;
> but time and chance happen to them all (Eccle-
> siastes 9:11).

Is there balance in your family's work, worship, rest,
and play? Why not talk about this as a family?

Consider it all joy *(James 1:2 NASB)*.

❧

I f you had to define joy, what would you say? And why is joy so important? One parent said, "I think joy is a good feeling. You know, when everything is right." Another parent said, "Joy is when you're adjusted." Yet another said, "Joy is the good life."

All of these answers focus on what is temporary. They're built on what we are doing or can do. What if there is no good feeling, or things just don't seem right, or there's no good life? Those things can be here today and gone tomorrow. Is it possible to have joy when there's not enough money to pay the bills or your child has been ill for a year? According to the word of God, yes.

Perhaps we could say joy is our response of faith as we look to God as our source of security—no matter what our circumstances. It's adopting God's perspective on what is going on in our lives. This is worth a try!

There was a man who had two sons. The younger
one said to his father, "Father, give me my
share of the estate." So he divided his property
between them...The older brother became
angry and refused to go in *(Luke 15:11-12,28)*.

～

We call this parable in Luke the story of the "Prodigal Son," but is that accurate? Couldn't it just as well be called the "Forgiving Father" or the "Older Critical Brother"? It's a portrayal of family relationships that applies to the present day. Here's a prayer by Ken Gire that brings the story home:

> Dear Beloved Son of the Father, how it must crush you when I turn my back on you and walk away...Thank you that although I have sometimes left home, I have never left your heart. Though I have forgotten about you, you have never forgotten about me...I confess that there is inside me not only a prodigal son but also a critical older brother...Gather both the prodigal part of myself and the critical part of myself in your loving arms, O Lord. And bring them home.[76]

[Love] always protects, always trusts, always
hopes, always perseveres *(1 Corinthians 13:7)*.

❦

To a Child About to Be Married

Here are some thoughts to help you walk the path-
way of marriage:

- Love is always doing. Love is always in
  motion. Love is the glue that holds our marriages together and the oil that keeps us
  from rubbing each other the wrong way...

- The strongest expression of love we can
  make is to sacrifice ourselves for one
  another...

- The deepest expression of our love comes
  through our willingness to share in the
  tedium of each other's daily routines and
  frustrations. When husband and wife are
  more focused on pleasing each other than
  getting their own way, God will free them
  to mutually love and respect each other...

- Nothing our spouse can do for us can touch
  us so deeply as faithfully praying for us day
  after day—long after another person would
  have moved on to something new.[77]

A patient man has great understanding, but a quick-tempered man displays folly (*Proverbs 14:29*).

<hr>

I'm so frustrated! That makes me mad!" We all have moments when our tempers flare. Three major culprits feed our frustration. One is our *expectations.* We all have them—for ourselves, our mates, our children, and even for our friends.

Another major cause of frustration is the *attitude of entitlement*—the simple belief that if I want something, I ought to have it.

The third culprit is the *belief that life should be fair.* We must recognize that life is not fair; that is a fact.

So, what can you do? One way to deal with frustration is to *internalize the guidelines from God's Word.* His guidelines for life are the best because they work. Here are two fundamental truths from Proverbs. Memorize them, practice them, and watch your frustration shrink:

> He who is slow to anger has great understanding, but he who is hasty of spirit exposes and exalts his folly (14:29 AMP).

> He who is slow to anger is better than the mighty, he who rules his [own] spirit than he who takes a city (16:32 AMP).

Now faith is being sure of what we hope for and
certain of what we do not see *(Hebrews 11:1).*

⊰⊱

I t's hard to trust my child now that he's into his teen
years." Some parents say that, and even more think it.
But let's consider this issue of trust for a moment. The
starting point in trusting your teenager is trust in God.
Why? There are three reasons.

First, parents who have come to know God's reliabil-
ity in their own lives can trust God to be working in the
lives of their teenagers.

Second, as parents learn to trust God in greater and
more intimate areas of their lives, they learn how to trust
people, including their teenagers. Even though teenagers
can be unreliable, God is still reliable.

Third, the parents' trust in God can be a model for
their teenagers to follow. The clearest picture of active
faith in God that teenagers will be able to see is their
parents trusting God in regard to them.

We do not have a high priest who is unable to
sympathize with our weaknesses, but we have
one who has been tempted in every way, just as
we are—yet was without sin *(Hebrews 4:15).*

❧

You worked from sunup to sundown making sure
every task was done. You tried to meet the needs of
every person. And then…you received a phone call and
were asked to do three more tasks. It wasn't so much the
requests that bothered you. It was the comment, "You're
not that busy, are you? You can work it in." You were ready
to scream! Nobody understood. You felt taken for granted,
used, unappreciated, and just plain exhausted.

That's the life of a parent. The problem is there's no
relief in sight. And it's the expectations other people have
of you that disturb you the most.

When no one understands you, it hurts. Sometimes
you may feel like saying, "Why bother?" You do and do
and do, and there's no appreciation. But here's some good
news: Guess who does understand? Guess who does care?
Jesus! Tell Him, ask Him, and then praise Him.

A friend loves at all times, and a brother is
born for adversity *(Proverbs 17:17)*.

❧

How do you respond to your children's friends? By
taking time, energy, and interest in your children's
friends, you are saying, "I love you" to your children. Your
offspring expect you to invest in them because they are
yours. But investing in their friends is an unexpected
bonus they'll appreciate. By taking an interest in their
friends...

> *You affirm your trust in their judgment.* And
> your trust is likely to be reciprocated.
>
> *You enhance your child's self-image.* Since
> he knows he has your trust, he has greater
> self-confidence and may exert a stronger influ-
> ence on them.
>
> *You build a climate of inclusion.* By investing
> in your children's friends, even those whom
> you find unattractive, you make it easy for
> them to include you rather than exclude you
> from their decisions.
>
> *You have a positive influence.* You make it
> easier for your children to lead their friends
> to Christ.

You are to give him the name Jesus, because he
will save his people from their sins *(Matthew 1:21)*.

～

The men's organization Promise Keepers used to host
meetings nationwide and as many as 50,000 to 75,000
would attend. Every so often during the meetings a chant
would break out that was quickly taken up by every man.
"Jesus, Jesus, Jesus" was shouted over and over again.

Hymnbooks abound with Jesus' name. How many
hymns can you recall with the name Jesus in the title?

And not only Christians say the name of Jesus. People
who don't believe in Him or know Him use His name
frequently.

Even though there are more than 100 different names
and titles given to Him, Jesus is His main one. Who
named Him? Did Jesus select His name? No. God said,
"Give him the name Jesus." Then God defined Jesus' purpose: "He will save his people from their sins." Some
people know, talk, teach, and preach about Him, yet still
miss out on knowing Him as Savior.[78]

Be kind and compassionate to one another,
forgiving each other, just as in Christ
God forgave you *(Ephesians 4:32).*

～～

W hat a verse to help a family! How can we apply it
in the daily interaction between a parent and child
or teenager? Here are some possibilities.

Cancel debts. Forgiving other people, just as God in
Christ has forgiven us, means cancelling the debts. It
means resisting the impulse to bring up the past.

Be kind. Webster's dictionary defines kindness as being
sympathetic, gentle, benevolent. Forgiveness springs much
easier from an attitude of kindness than from an attitude
of defensiveness. When we feel threatened, we tend to
become defensive. Replacing defensiveness with kindness
means we become vulnerable to being taken advantage
of again.

Be tenderhearted. Being tenderhearted implies even
more vulnerability. It means absorbing some hurt so our
children can grow. The opposite of tenderheartedness
is hardness of heart. Tenderhearted people can forgive.
This also applies to parent–child relationships. It takes
tenderhearted, forgiving parents to develop tenderhearted,
forgiving children and teenagers.

We love one another *(2 John 1:5).*

⊰⊱

Paul Lewis, the founder of Dad's University, a ministry to fathers, has made many practical suggestions for fathers. Some of these can be applied to mothers as well.

- If you're going away on a business trip, you may want to record some bedtime stories for your children to listen to while you're gone. If the stories you read are from books, leave the books so your children can follow along.

- Some evening, have all the family members switch places at the dinner table. During the meal, they need to talk and behave just like the family member whose chair they're sitting in. Get ready for an educational experience!

- Some parents take photos of their children doing things right and post the pictures somewhere in the house during the week.

- Some fathers plan out how they will greet each family member when they arrive home from work.

Take a moment now to put your creative talents to work and develop some additional creative ideas.[79] Put the words "I love you" into action.

Practice what you have learned and received
and heard and seen in me, and model your
way of living on it *(Philippians 4:9 AMP)*.

When your child becomes a teenager, your role as a parent changes. That's the only way to survive, but it's also beneficial. In fact, one of the best ways we can restructure our relationships with our teenagers is to begin building two-way accountability.

In two-way accountability, a dad would be willing to go to his teenage son and say, "Son, I'm working on not being anxious and committing everything to God in prayer. I'd like to report my progress to you each evening, and I'd like you to ask me how I'm doing. I'd like you to suggest ways I can learn quicker. And when you notice me getting anxious about something, I'd like you to remind me to commit it to the Lord right away. Okay?"

What do you think about this? When a parent initiates two-way accountability, he or she gives the teen a positive model that will make change and growth easier to accomplish.

[The Lord said] to me, "My grace is sufficient for you, for my power is made perfect in weakness." Therefore I will boast all the more gladly about my weaknesses, so that Christ's power may rest on me *(2 Corinthians 12:9)*.

D o you ever feel as if you're living your life in a courtroom? You're not in the jury box, though, nor the judge's bench, nor at the table where the attorneys sit. You're on the stand. You're standing trial!

Some people seem to go from one trial to another. As one parent cried out, "Trials! Who needs them?" We all do. Trials are an educational experience, though there may be times when we wish we didn't have to face them. Chuck Swindoll offers an excellent perspective on the purpose of trials:

> Trials are designed for us, not for our surroundings. God wishes to train us, to mold us. He uses the distressing circumstances of life as His tools. He allows the icy feelings of despondency to linger within us. In doing so, He deals bountifully with us... deep within where no one else can see or touch.[80]

The teaching of the wise is a fountain of life, that one
may avoid the snares of death *(Proverbs 13:14 AMP)*.

～⚶～

Have you ever flown in a helicopter? What's amazing
about this machine is that it can climb straight up,
hover in one spot, and dart around in different directions
like a giant fly. Helicopters are used to take people into
the depths of a volcano crater to see the sights.

Helicopters make a lot of wind and noise. They're
not noted for going fast. But they have a job to do. They
hover, rescue, and protect. Some parents are like helicopters. They hover overhead to provide constant protection.
Perhaps you've seen them. They pick up all the slack for
their children. Why do they do this? They say it's because
they love their children.

These parents won't allow their children to fail. That's
sad. Failure is one of the greatest learning experiences
of life. When you do something wrong, it provides you
with the opportunity to know how to do it right the
next time.

If we rescue our children from failure now, someday
they will really fail and we won't be there. And they won't
know how to handle it. Let them learn now so they can
be prepared later.[81]

The prayer of a righteous man is powerful
and effective *(James 5:16)*.

～❧～

Sometimes the obstacles to the spiritual and emotional
well-being of our children are present not just in us as
parents, but also in other members of the family.

Prayer for Healing of the Family Tree

God, the Father, Almighty, Creator of all
  beings…
We know that since the fall…our family
  ancestry includes
not only talents and virtues but also much
  tragedy and sin.
Today…I ask that You would heal our family
  tree.
I call to mind each member of the family…
and I ask for Your healing graces to bless
  him (her)…
Especially, I beg You, loving God,
to cleanse me of any bad patterns
coming from my family background…
Come, O Holy Spirit, to teach us
how to mingle necessary sacrifice with
  proper self-love,
that we may be able to respond to the needs
  of our babies
in ways that are prudent and sound.[82]

> Do your best to present yourself to God as
> one approved, a workman who does not
> need to be ashamed and who correctly
> handles the word of truth *(2 Timothy 2:15).*

~∞~

You're in the doctor's office waiting with your child. The doctor takes out a needle and carefully injects the contents into the arm of your wide-eyed child. While the shot may have hurt momentarily, it is of important and lasting consequence. Your child was just inoculated against a life-threatening disease. In the shot, your child was given a small dose of the disease. This weakened form triggered the body's immune system in a way that activated its forces and built some antibodies to fight off the disease.

The best way to help your children develop the character they need is to inoculate them against what they will encounter. Don't keep your children in a protected hothouse environment. Expose them gradually, bit by bit, to problems and stresses. While you're doing it, talk with them and show them how to handle what they are going to encounter. That way they're better prepared and not thrown off course.

Since the day we heard about you, we have not
stopped praying for you and asking God to fill you
with the knowledge of his will through all spiritual
wisdom and understanding *(Colossians 1:9)*.

Oⁿe of the most frequent questions parents ask is,
"How should I pray for my children when they're
in trouble?" But the other side of the coin is, "What's the
best way to pray for my children when they're doing well
and living for the Lord?" We can pray,

> Dear Lord, I bring my children to You.
> They have heard the Word of God which
> I have taught them, and they have believed.
> Now keep them, protect them by the power
> of Your name, Lord Jesus Christ. Don't let
> the Evil One steal away the teaching they
> have received, but rather let it grow in them.
> Make them mighty men and women of
> God to Your honor and glory.[83]

How will you pray for your family today?

We love because he first loved us *(1 John 4:19)*.

❧

I s there love in your family? Is there affection in your family? But why ask about love and affection in two different questions? Aren't they the same? No, not really. We're supposed to love one another. This love comes as a sense of family duty and loyalty. But liking one another… that's something else. Kent and Barbara Hughes suggest there are three elements to growing in affection. The first is *loving God,* because it connects you with the source of love (1 John 4:8). It also empowers you to love (1 John 4:19).

The second element is *loving each other.* Children need the assurance of their parents' love for one another.

The third element for family affection comes through *clear communication.* It involves adapting what you say so the other person can accept and understand it. And both ears and eyes must be involved in listening.

Building family affection…is not a chore, it's a pleasure.[84]

The father of a righteous man has great joy;
he who has a wise son delights in him. May
your father and mother be glad; may she who
gave you birth rejoice! *(Proverbs 23:24-25).*

A s they go through life, your children are going to be
faced with a multitude of decisions. Will they say
yes or no to drugs? Will they say yes or no to premarital
sex? Will they say yes or no to an attractive cult leader?
Will they say yes or no to the wrong person to marry?
There will be times when they, like you, will need insight,
wisdom, and help.

What if they end up just drifting through school or
into some job with little or no meaning? What if they
never tap into and activate the potential that God has
given to them? What if...?

Now isn't the time to ask, "What if...?" Right decisions come from wisdom and discernment. Read, study,
and memorize God's Word. Pray for wisdom for you
and your child.

Fathers, do not exasperate your children;
instead, bring them up in the training and
instruction of the Lord *(Ephesians 6:4)*.

～

Fathering is tough. It's on-the-job learning with insufficient time for just trying to keep up with the kids, the payments, and life itself. In a national survey, dads were asked to describe their feelings about fathering using word pictures:

"I feel like a duck out of water."

"I feel like a loved teddy bear with all the fuzz rubbed off."

"I feel like the sun on a partly cloudy day, warm and nice when it's there, but not there quite as much as my children would like."

"I feel like I'm swimming against a river of things that are demanding my time, struggling to get to the island where my children are waiting."

"I feel like water in the shower, which runs hot and cold depending on who is using water in other parts of the house."[85]

As a parent, how would you describe, in word pictures, what you're doing?

Confess your sins to each other and pray for each other so that you may be healed. The prayer of a righteous man is powerful and effective *(James 5:16)*.

⤳

Sometimes songs convey our thoughts better than anything else, as does this excerpt from a song for a child called "Above All Else" by Michael and Stormie Omartian.

> If I had my way, I'd keep you safe within my arms
> While the storm of life crashes.
> I won't always be with you, my child, but words
>   I can give.
> When the winds of hope are dying down, these
>   words will live.
> Above all else, know God's the One who'll
>   never leave you.
> Look to Him above all else.
> He is love you can depend upon, a heart set
>   to care.
> If in the darkest night you should be lost,
>   He will be there...
> He's the Author of your laughter,
> He's the Keeper of your tears,
> He's the One who you must fear
> Above all else...
> Just love the Lord above all else.[86]

Even to your old age and gray hairs I am he, I
am he who will sustain you *(Isaiah 46:4)*.

Y ou're growing older, aren't you? We don't really like to
admit it. We live in a society that celebrates the vitality
of youth. But we all hit our thirties, forties, fifties, sixties,
and beyond. If we don't hit them, it's because...well, we
know the alternative.

We have a condition in this country described as "the
graying of America." More and more people are in their
sixties. How we face and handle aging is an education
for our children. We can take the pessimistic approach or
the biblical approach. Old age can be a time of strength,
as reflected in Isaiah 46:4. We can live in the past and
dread our future or look toward the future and live with
faith and hope.

Have you ever considered that there just might be joy
in aging? Psalm 92:14 says, "[The righteous] will still bear
fruit in old age, they will stay fresh and green."[87]

Instead, it should be that of your inner self, the unfading beauty of a gentle and quiet spirit, which is of great worth in God's sight *(1 Peter 3:4)*.

Have you ever had one of those days where you've got a case of the blahs? You're not feeling up, you're not down—you're just feeling *blah*. Years ago there was a movie called *Ordinary People*. We don't like to feel ordinary. Do you like being known as an ordinary parent with an ordinary spouse and ordinary children? Ordinary never seems to end.

We all want to be unique, special, unusual, or even spectacular. But why? What will that do for us? Where will it get us? And more importantly, who sets the standard for what or who is special? You? The world? God?

God already sees you as special because you are His creation. Every little, unassuming, ordinary, faithful step you take and task you fulfill is pleasing to your heavenly Father. And when you please Him, do you know what happens? The ordinary turns into the extraordinary!

Arise, cry out in the night, as the watches of the
night begin; pour out your heart like water in
the presence of the Lord *(Lamentations 2:19)*.

Whenever you apply for a job, you usually ask if you
can look at the job description. You want to know
what to expect and what you'll be doing with your time.
That's a wise step to take because you want to make sure
the job is right for you. As a parent, you might find it
helpful to draw up a job description of the task of parenting. Stormie Omartian wrote,

> We try to do the best we can raising our
> children. Then, just when we think we've
> got the parenting terrain all figured out,
> we suddenly find ourselves in new territory
> again as each new age and stage presents
> another set of challenges.[88]

What makes the difference? Prayer. Praying specifically for each child. When Jesus Christ is your resource
and your source of strength as a parent, let the problems come. You're not alone. Knowing that can be a real
source of calm.

Why is life given to a man whose way is hidden,
whom God has hedged in? *(Job 3:23)*.

~~~

Children are constantly asking, "Why?" But so are adults. Especially when circumstances go wrong. We ask that question of ourselves, other people, and even God. Don't worry, you won't be the last person to ask God why. And you're definitely not the first. Many years ago, one of God's prophets asked Him the same question because he was appalled by all the suffering he saw, just as some of us are pained by what we see today.

When we encounter the deep valleys in our lives, they soon reflect our theology and philosophy of life. Many Christians believe, for example, that life is (or ought to be) fair. They think, *If I'm a Christian, I should be immune to tragedy.* God does not insulate us from misfortunes, however, and He never promised He would.

Hard times are opportunities to become more dependent upon God and discover that even when things don't go our way, we will still survive. These are learning experiences for us.

Even a child is known by his actions, by whether
his conduct is pure and right *(Proverbs 20:11)*.

❧

What kind of reputation do you want your children to have? A label or series of descriptive adjectives, once applied, seems to stick to us like superglue. Most parents want their children to be known for doing what is right. But the question is, by whose standards? There are many sets of values in operation in our world today.

The Bible is the standard that Christian parents want their children to follow. That standard can be summed up in one word: purity. Not only does Proverbs talk about that, but so did Paul. He said, "Keep yourself pure" (1 Timothy 5:22). That's hard because it means you have to go counterculture. And if you think it's difficult for an adult to do that, imagine what it must be like for a child. You see, being pure means being free from anything that taints, impairs, or infects—free from defects and sin. That's asking a lot! But prayer will make a difference!

A cheerful heart is good medicine, but a crushed
spirit dries up the bones *(Proverbs 17:22)*.

❧

Tim Hansel has some great insights on humor:

Humor is one of the most powerful influences
in a family. It can be used very effectively in
discipline. We're called to discipline our kids,
not punish them. The word *discipline* actually means "to learn." It doesn't mean to put
chains on our kids...

Humor is a miracle substance for families.
It's easy to overreact when our kids make mistakes, but if we learn not to take ourselves
too seriously, they will find it easier to correct
their errors...

Laughter is so important that I've made it a
high priority. John Powell once said, "He who
learns to laugh at himself shall never cease to
be entertained." We need to learn to laugh at
ourselves, because the human predicament is
so notoriously difficult. Life can be so prepos-
terously hard that if we didn't learn to laugh at
ourselves, we wouldn't survive. Families today
are going through more stress than ever before,
but a well-developed sense of humor can keep
them from breaking.[89]

In the same way, the Spirit helps us in our weakness.
We do not know what we ought to pray for, but
the Spirit himself intercedes for us with groans
that words cannot express *(Romans 8:26)*.

~~~

Have you ever been at a loss for words? That happens
to all of us at one time or another. Someone gives
you an unexpected outrageous compliment in front of
other people and your mind goes into space. What do
you say?

Or your children have misbehaved all day long and
now you've hit the last straw with them. Your brain freezes
and the choice words that you want to spit out just don't
come out.

But these aren't the only places where we've been at
a loss. It happens when we pray too. However, there is
one difference when you talk with God. Someone else
is helping and speaking for you when you're at a loss for
words. The Holy Spirit knows how to express what is
bottled up within you that can't be translated into words.
He'll speak for you.

Be strong and very courageous. Be careful to
obey all the law my servant Moses gave you; do
not turn from it to the right or to the left, that you
may be successful wherever you go *(Joshua 1:7)*.

The words the Lord gave to Joshua on how to be a successful leader are applicable for you as parents because you are the leaders of your family. (Read Joshua 1:7-9.)

First, there is the promise of the *presence of God* in your life. Second, the Lord said Joshua didn't need to be afraid or dismayed. God wouldn't fail him. We too are promised the same *protection of God.* The third promise is the *provision of God.*

Joshua was also promised the *power of God.* God said Joshua would receive the power he needed to lead as long as he obeyed the Word of God. Families that look to the Word of God as their source of guidance and insight will find stability.

Joshua was promised the presence, the protection, the provision, and the power of God. The same promises have been given to you!

Better a patient man than a warrior, a man who controls
his temper than one who takes a city *(Proverbs 16:32)*.

～

I get angry as a parent—is that wrong? Is that a sin?"
Does Scripture label anger as a sin? No, it doesn't.
Unfortunately, we sometimes respond to the emotion
of anger in ways that *lead* to sin. That is one reason why
both the Old and New Testaments teach us to be slow
to anger (see also James 1:19).

The starting point for the positive use of anger is to
understand that it is a God-given emotion. Anger is not
an evil or destructive emotion in itself. Anger isn't necessarily dangerous. The real problem is the mismanagement
and misunderstanding of it—the emotional immaturity
of the individual who allows himself or herself to be controlled by anger energy.

We can't always control when or how we experience
anger. However, with God's help, we can learn to control
how we choose to interpret and express that emotion.[90]

Jesus answered her, "If you knew the gift of
God and who it is that asks you for a drink,
you would have asked him and he would
have given you living water" *(John 4:10).*

❧

You've been walking for hours in the desert. It's hot,
dry, and dusty. The land is parched and so is your
mouth. All you can think about is water—cool, wet,
thirst-quenching water poured into your mouth. You may
have had such an experience. Most of the time, however,
we have sufficient water for our needs.

We all need water. We can live without food for 10 to
15 days. But three days without water can be a disaster.
We who are Christians have been given another type of
water: Jesus, the fountain of life. Scripture describes us
as being conveyers of water too. Jesus said, "Whoever
believes in me, as the Scripture has said, streams of living
water will flow from within him" (John 7:38). We are
called to be rivers of blessing![91]

You will seek me and find me when you seek
me with all your heart *(Jeremiah 29:13)*.

~~~

As parents, there's a game we all end up playing with our children. It's called hide-and-seek. Kids love it. But it's a game for kids...not for adults.

Sometimes adults continue to play hide-and-seek, but the results aren't so much fun. Parents hide themselves from their children—they hide their time, love, feelings, or personal involvement. There are problems when adults engage in this activity.

Husbands and wives can engage in a marital game of hide-and-seek too. Often the person hiding or distancing him- or herself from the other partner never stops in one place long enough to get caught.

Some adults play a perpetual game of hide-and-seek with God. They look for God halfheartedly and say, "He's not around. I can't find Him."

With God being who He is, how could we ever really hide from Him? It's odd...why would we want to hide from someone who loves us so much and wants the best for us? I wonder...

Now that I, your Lord and Teacher, have
washed your feet, you also should wash
one another's feet *(John 13:14)*.

⊱⊰

L ife involves a constant change of roles. Perhaps it's happened in your family. The person who was the main
wage earner is now the one taking care of the home and
the former homemaker is the wage earner.

When you were younger, your parents took care of
you. If it hasn't happened yet, there may come a time
when you will become a parent to your parents and care
for them. And your children, whom you cared for, may
end up reversing roles with you in a number of years.
Scary thought, isn't it? But that's life. We all experience
role changes. Fortunately, Jesus experienced a role change
too.

In Philippians 2:7, Paul says that Christ, who was equal
with God, who in fact was God, "made Himself nothing,
taking the very nature of a servant." More than that, "He
humbled Himself and became obedient to death—even
death on a cross!"[92]

He who covers and forgives an offense seeks
love, but he who repeats or harps on a matter
separates even close friends *(Proverbs 17:9 AMP)*.

～✦～

A re your parents still living? If so, how is your relationship with them? And even if they are deceased,
how is your relationship? (Many deceased parents still
exert a tremendous amount of control over their living
children. Often you still hear their voices, experience
their training, reflect on their values, or even feel inhib-
ited in your life because of something they did or said.) If
there are any problems or residual effects that still affect
you because of your parents, the solution just may be to
forgive them.

The reason this is important is because it will not only
help you, but also your children. They will know if there
is a problem between you and your parents. And they
will learn from your example. If there is no residue of
bad feelings from your parents, praise the Lord. If there
is, forgive them, and you'll become free to praise the
Lord in a new way.

Train yourself to be godly *(1 Timothy 4:7)*.

⌇

N ow I'm going to meddle a bit in another area of life. Do you have a regular aerobic exercise program that you follow, say, at least three to four times per week? When you walk up two flights of stairs, does your heart rate stay the same or is it racing?

We live in a world that is health-conscious, an age of physical fitness. But there's another kind of fitness that's even better. It's called spiritual fitness. It's easy to become so busy that it, like physical fitness, can be neglected. Physical fitness helps us in this life. Spiritual fitness helps us even more so in this life, but also for eternity.

If your child were to ask you, "How can I stay spiritually fit?" what would you say? Spiritual fitness will happen when we:

- Spend time each day in prayer—praising, adoring, asking, interceding.

- Spend time each day in worship—this can occur in your home as well as at church.

- Spend time in your local church serving and ministering to others.

Children's children are a crown to the aged, and
parents are the pride of their children *(Proverbs 17:6).*

⊰⊱

What did you call your father? Everyone has different names for their dad, some formal and some
informal. Sometimes when a child reaches adulthood he
or she calls Father by his first name. Others continue to
call him Daddy. Chuck Swindoll shares some memories
about his own father:

> My dad has not always been "Pop" to
> us. We, my brothers and sister, as well as
> mom, called him "Daddy" when we were
> young...Looking back, I can see that my
> parents, by joint effort, have done an excep-
> tionally good job raising us. High moral
> values, spiritual priorities, academic excel-
> lence—all these have been held out to us
> as important. My pop has instilled in us
> kids a sense of trust. He's been available,
> especially in emergencies. He has done
> what he thinks best for us, even when we
> might not agree—as an example, in the
> business world, our family, our church. My
> dad has a corner on the upper echelons of
> fatherhood.[93]

So I tell you this, and insist on it in the Lord, that
you must no longer live as the Gentiles do, in
the futility of their thinking *(Ephesians 4:17)*.

A sk your children, "How are you?" and often you get
an automatic, nonthinking response of "Fine." But
if you want a puzzled look and rapt attention, ask them,
"How's your mind today?" They may look at you like
you've lost yours!

The condition of our minds may be more important
than how our bodies feel. What happens in your mind,
and your children's, can make or break an entire day.
Your thoughts can determine your feelings and even the
health of your body.

How are you using your mind in relationship to God?
What do you think about? What goes on inside your
head when you read the Scripture and it tells you to do
something that is different from what you've been doing?
We're called to obedience. God wants us to think about
what He is saying in His Word and to discover the benefits of following it.

The Son of Man did not come to be served, but to serve, and to give his life as a ransom for many *(Matthew 20:28)*.

～

A parent sitting in church one day heard the pastor read today's verse. Because she had a particularly draining week, her first response was, "I don't think I'm being sacrilegious, but there are days when I feel that way. Serve, serve, serve. That's all I do!" Perhaps you have also felt that way at times. Think for a moment what you experience each day.

Do you laugh? Jesus laughed.

Do you cry? Oh, He wept.

Do you get tired? So did He.

How about hunger? He knew the contractions of an empty stomach. What about thirst? Yes, of course. Especially when He was hanging on the cross.

Have you ever suffered? He did in many ways.

You haven't died...yet. He did in a very painful manner.

The Son of God became the Son of Man that we might become sons and daughters of God.

My son, do not make light of the Lord's discipline, and
do not lose heart when he rebukes you, because
the Lord disciplines those he loves, and he punishes
everyone he accepts as a son *(Hebrews 12:5-6)*.

Some parents violate God's pattern by failing to discipline. You don't show love or do your children a favor when you neglect to discipline them. Hebrews 12:11 says, "No discipline seems pleasant at the time, but painful. Later on, however, it produces a harvest of righteousness and peace for those who have been trained by it." There is a purpose for discipline.

As a parent you really don't have the option *not* to discipline. It's a duty, but it's also a privilege. A time of correction is an opportunity to train, educate, and demonstrate love. Make it a learning experience. Don't take all the responsibility upon yourself to explain. Ask your child what happened, what the consequences ought to be, and what he or she will do differently the next time. It may make a difference in all of your lives.

Give thanks in all circumstances, for this is God's
will for you in Christ Jesus *(1 Thessalonians 5:18).*

*A*ttitude. What is it? It's a choice we make to look at life
in a certain way. It determines the atmosphere of our
homes and the way we interact with people. Some people
claim they were born with a gloomy disposition. Perhaps
some of your children seem to have been born with an
abundance of gratitude genes whereas other children seem
to be shortchanged. Some have a sore disposition whereas
others can be ridiculously cheerful and grateful.

Yet we don't inherit gratitude genes from our parents.
We choose to display gratitude. We can choose to be
thankful and look for the best and the blessings rather
than the defects. We can make a choice to search, discover,
and not take for granted what we have or experience.

We teach our children to say "Thank you." It's even
more important to teach them to thank God for all that
we are, all that we have, and all that we delight in.

Be very careful, then, how you live—not as unwise but
as wise, making the most of every opportunity, because
the days are evil. Therefore do not be foolish, but
understand what the Lord's will is *(Ephesians 5:15-17)*.

ou're wasting time." Perhaps you grew up hearing that
phrase again and again. For some of us it stuck in our
minds and became a guilt-prodding stimulus that still
exerts its control today. For others, it had no impact what-
soever. Somewhere there's got to be a balance.

Perhaps you make good use of your time and are dil-
igent and hard-working. The real issue, however, is not
how you make use of your time. You can be busy and
still not do much. It's *what* you do that has value. Paul
said to "make the *most* of your time."

Have you ever asked the other members of your family,
"What did you do of value today?" Try it. You'll also want
to look back over the last seven days and ask yourself that
same question for each day.

Moses built an altar and called it The LORD is my Banner.
He said, "For hands were lifted up to the throne of the
LORD. The LORD will be at war against the Amalekites
from generation to generation" *(Exodus 17:15-16)*.

During a battle, Moses was on a hill praying to the
Lord. As long as his arms were lifted up in prayer,
Israel was winning. But just like us, his arms got tired,
and when he dropped them the Amalekites began to win.
So Aaron and Hur came over and held up his arms as he
prayed. The result? Israel won.

There are different ways we can support and help one
another. When our spouse or child is feeling down or
exhausted, we can give him or her a back rub. We can
ask other family members how they would like us to
pray for them during the day. We can let them know
that we're holding them up in prayer even when they
don't request it.

As a family, who can you hold up in prayer?

Even to your old age and gray hairs I am he, I
am he who will sustain you *(Isaiah 46:4)*.

〜

Weary? Frazzled? Worn out? Children get this way
and need the arms of their mother or father. Parents get this way and also need another person's arms.
Consider this:

> On one of my draggy, dreary days God showed
> me that He [carries me like a child]. Even
> though my gray hairs now outnumber the
> brown, God still cares for me as His child...I
> grabbed a pen and paper and scribbled:
>
> > God *upholds* me when I am about to fall.
> >
> > When I am despondent and discouraged,
> > He's the "lifter of my head."
> >
> > He *carries* me when I have no strength of
> > my own, when I am helpless, and for
> > all of my life—from birth to death.
> >
> > He *sustains* me when I am weary, worn
> > out, when those I love can't, when
> > friends turn away, when support systems collapse.
> >
> > He *rescues* me when fear overtakes me,
> > when enemies surround me.
> >
> > What a fantastic Father![94]

A patient man has great understanding, but a quick-tempered man displays folly *(Proverbs 14:29)*.

⋙

H ave you ever...

- waited in line at the bank for ten minutes only to discover that the person immediately in front of you has a stack of business deposits and receipts to reconcile with the bank teller?

- waited in the grocery line when the person in front of you pulls out 200 coupons to wade through?

Yes! Welcome to life in the fast lane! We fuss, fume, fret, and flip out over "minor" daily occurrences like these. How can a parent or anyone handle these unexpected delays? The answer is in the question—the unexpected. Always expect the unexpected. That's not being pessimistic, but realistic. Life will not always go the way you think it should. Begin each day by saying, "Something is not going to go the way I want it to go today, and that's all right. I can handle it." Then when the unexpected happens, you're ready for it.

I will do whatever you ask in my name, so that the
Son may bring glory to the Father. You may ask me for
anything in my name, and I will do it *(John 14:13-14)*.

～

When you pray for your children, do you also pray
for yourself? Sometimes the changes we pray for
in our children don't materialize because we're not seek-
ing some needed changes in our own lives. Consider this
from *The Power of a Praying Parent*:

> Lord,
>   I submit myself to You...I know I need
> You to help me. I want to partner with You
> and partake of Your gifts of wisdom, discern-
> ment, revelation, and guidance. I also need
> Your strength and patience, along with a gen-
> erous portion of Your love flowing through
> me. Teach me how to love the way You love...
> Make me the parent You want me to be and
> teach me how to pray and truly intercede for
> the life of this child...In Jesus' name I ask
> that You will increase my faith to believe for
> all the things You've put on my heart to pray
> for concerning this child.[95]

Forgetting what is behind and straining toward what is
ahead, I press on toward the goal *(Philippians 3:13-14).*

⤝

The past. What do you do with it? Or what do you let it
do to you? We think about what happened yesterday
with the children, or less recently during our adolescent
years, or even back to our own dealings with our parents.
And sometimes we feel regret. We say, "If only I had…"
or "Oh, how I regret…" or, "If only I could have done it
differently I wouldn't be in this plight today."

There is a place for regret—once! And then we must
begin moving in a new direction. Instead of dragging
along the unnecessary baggage of regret, blame, and
renunciation, have you ever tried *rejoicing* over the past?
That may sound strange, but rejoicing eventually brings
release.

Eventually, your children will need to learn how to
deal with their pasts. How they see you handling your
past will be a model for them. What a wonderful opportunity you have to teach them *how* rather than *why*.

The law was given through Moses; grace and
truth came through Jesus Christ *(John 1:17)*.

❧

Rules, rules, rules. We all have to live by them to
a certain extent. Our society wouldn't be able to
function without rules. As a parent, you're the creator
and enforcer of certain rules in your household. Unfortunately, in some families people go to the extreme with
rules. They make life restrictive and burdensome, and
live in a self-imposed bondage. And they expect others
to do likewise. This becomes legalism.

Fortunately, the Christian life is one lived by grace. To
understand grace, you need to know about an old Hebrew
term that means "to bend or to stoop." Eventually it came
to encompass the idea of "condescending favor."[96]

> To show grace is to extend favor or kind-
> ness to one who doesn't deserve it and can
> never earn it. Receiving God's acceptance
> by grace always stands in sharp contrast to
> earning it on the basis of works…Favor is
> being extended simply out of the goodness
> of the heart of the giver.[97]

He did right in the sight of the Lord and walked in all
the ways of David his [forefather], and turned not
aside to the right hand or to the left *(2 Kings 22:2 AMP)*.

※

This verse is talking about a man by the name of Josiah, who came from a dysfunctional family. In fact, he came from a family that was dysfunctional for generations. His parents, grandparents, and relatives were idolators, sorcerers, and murderers. That is the legacy Josiah brought with him to the throne when he became king. But he didn't let that influence him. He chose to turn that around. He left a positive legacy as evidenced by today's verse.

All of us will leave a legacy. Some of that legacy will be etched on our tombstones, and some of it on other people's hearts. "But true epitaphs are not carved in stone. They are carved in the souls and memories of men and women, boys and girls."[98]

Why not write your own epitaph…and then live up to it?

Come, all you who are thirsty, come to the
waters; and you who have no money, come,
buy and eat! Come, buy wine and milk without
money and without cost *(Isaiah 55:1).*

✧

"Mom...Mom...Mother! I'm thirsty!" "Daddy...
Daddy! I need you...now!" You've heard it before.
You'll hear it again. The cry of a child who has a basic
need that requires fulfillment. You have some of the same
needs, the same longings. You were born with these God-
given longings.

All of us, including our children, desire to be wanted
by another person. We want to be valued by another. We
want to be accepted for who we are rather than what we
do. We want to be loved with no conditions and no reservations. We want to belong. That's a tall order!

Where are the people who can do all that? Where are
the spouses, the parents, the children who can fit this
description? They're nonexistent...except in our fantasies.
The only one who can do all this is God.[99]

After the Feast was over, while his parents were returning home, the boy Jesus stayed behind in Jerusalem, but they were unaware of it *(Luke 2:43)*.

~~~

Have you ever left your child somewhere, thinking that he or she was with your spouse or someone else? It happened to Jesus' parents. Imagine not being able to find your child for three or four days. What would go through your mind?

Then they found Him. He was sitting in the temple teaching the teachers.

Jesus, our Savior, started out as a baby much like all other babies. But He was different as a boy. When He sat and talked with some of the brightest minds of the day in the temple, they were amazed. And His parents were astonished. It seems as if a new side of their son was revealed that day.

That's the way it is when you're a parent. Your baby becomes a child, then a teenager, and finally an adult. Each stage brings you opportunities to be astonished. How have your children astonished you?[100]

God will redeem my life from the grave; he
will surely take me to himself *(Psalm 49:15)*.

～✦～

Have you ever done anything wrong? Of course. Have
your children? Definitely! Will they continue to do
wrong things? Yes, they will. What is one way we respond
when we say or do something we know we shouldn't have
done? When we make an error we try to make up for it.

The Word of God sometimes calls sin "error" or "errors":
"Who can discern his errors? Forgive my hidden faults"
(Psalm 19:12). Some people don't like the word *sin,* so they
call their misdeeds mistakes, mishaps, or even errors. But
it's all the same. The problem is that when it comes to sin,
we can't make up for it. That's the bad news. The good
news, however, is that Jesus can make up for it. He has
covered us with His blood. Our redemption is complete,
and we can rest in that thought the rest of our lives![101]

For God so loved the world that he gave his one
and only Son, that whoever believes in him shall
not perish but have eternal life *(John 3:16)*.

~✦~

Several kinds of love are mentioned in Scripture. There
is *eros,* the romantic kind of love that gives you funny
feelings in your stomach. And there's *storge,* the love that
we experience for our family members. And of course
there's *phileo,* which is known as friendship love. The
sacrificial love Jesus modeled for us is called *agape.* It's an
unselfish love that gives of itself and doesn't expect anything back. Of course, that's easy to say and hard to do.

Agape is the love that grows and expands as you give
it. It's the unconditional love God gives us regardless of
who we are or what we've done. It's not natural to love
this way. We want others to deserve our love. But does
anyone ever really deserve love? No, because we're all
inconsistent. How do you make agape love part of your
life? Like the old Nike ad said, "Just do it."[102]

Blessed are the peacemakers, for they will
be called sons of God *(Matthew 5:9)*.

꙳

D o you want a peaceful home? So many parents cry
out, "If only we could get along and have peace
between the kids!" or "All I want is some peace and quiet!"
Many homes are characterized more by warfare than by
peace and mutual love. Peace, in the Bible, doesn't just
mean freedom from all trouble. Rather, it means focusing on and promoting everything that is beneficial and
good. Peace means overcoming hostility.

Most people say they love peace. But Scripture says,
"Blessed are the *peacemakers*," not just the peace lovers.
How can you bring peace into your family? Consider
these words from Paul: "Do not repay anyone evil for
evil. Be careful to do what is right in the eyes of everybody. If it is possible, as far as it depends on you, live at
peace with everyone" (Romans 12:17-18).

Sometimes we allow ourselves to be drawn into the
same behavior that's shown by the other person. Don't
retaliate. There's a better way, and you can model it.

You, my brothers, were called to be free. But do
not use your freedom to indulge the sinful nature;
rather, serve one another in love *(Galatians 5:13)*.

〰️

S ometimes getting information from the horse's mouth
will give us the best advice and guidance. Read what
Bart Campolo said about how his parents helped him
grow:

> That's what real freedom is, I think: the under-
> standing that in a world filled with choices
> and decisions, under tremendous pressure from
> other people and our own desires, amid the
> paralyzing fear of mistakes or failure, loving
> God and loving His people are the only things
> that really matter, and doing those things is a
> decision that we genuinely have the ability to
> make in every situation.
>
> You and Mom didn't let me do whatever I
> wanted to, Dad, but you gave me my freedom
> nonetheless. I think I finally appreciate it.[103]

Love, Bart

Children's children are a crown to the aged, and
parents are the pride of their children *(Proverbs 17:6)*.

⌇⌇⌇

That's my dad." "That's my mom. She's the second one
from the left, with the funny hat on." "My dad is the
greatest fisherman in our family." These are statements of
pride coming from the mouths of children.

What qualities or abilities do your parents have that
you're proud about? To be proud of another person means
you have delight or satisfaction in who that person is or
what he or she has achieved. It's all right to be proud of
people. It begins early in life with our children. We take
pride in our children's expressions, first steps, ability to
read, and so on.

But what qualities in your life can your child be proud
about? It could be an achievement, your position at church
or in the community, or an ability. But what about pride
over what you believe, what you stand for, your values,
and the way you are consistent and fair in your love and
response to your children? These actually have more value
for your children's lives.

Even a child is known by his actions, by whether
his conduct is pure and right *(Proverbs 20:11).*

How would you describe your own reputation? You
have one, you know. So does each member of your
family. Do you know what *reputation* means? According
to *Webster's New World Dictionary*, it means "the esti-
mation in which a person or thing is commonly held,
whether favorable or not."

Parents can help their children develop their reputations by what they do and say. We see this in 1 Timothy
4:12: "Don't let anyone look down on you because you
are young, but set an example for the believers in speech,
in life, in love, in faith and in purity."

As parents it's OK to be concerned about our children's reputations. But there's another reputation to be
more concerned about—your own. That's because it has
a direct effect on your children's reputations. Paul urges
us to handle ourselves so that the way we live will always
be "worthy of the Lord and may please him in every way:
bearing fruit in every good work, growing in the knowledge of God" (Colossians 1:10).[104]

A fool shows his annoyance at once, but a prudent
man overlooks an insult (*Proverbs 12:16*).

"I'm insulted by that comment." We've all felt the sting
of an insult. It hurts. It cuts. And it's even worse when
it comes from another family member. The place where
life ought to be the safest is often the riskiest—the home.
We cut loose at home more than we do elsewhere. All it
takes is a bit of sarcasm to unleash a counterattack, and
soon it's a matter of who can top who. Why is the home
so vulnerable to attack?

First, in the family, you know each other so well that
you know where to jab. Another reason we attack each
other is because we know we can get away with it. You
can't resign from your family or fire family members.
A third reason the home is so vulnerable is because we
live in a society in which humor is built around insults
and sarcasm.

There's a better way to relate as a family, and Peter
described it: "Finally, all of you, live in harmony with one
another; be sympathetic, love as brothers, be compassionate and humble. Do not repay evil with evil or insult with
insult, but with blessing, because to this you were called
so that you may inherit a blessing" (1 Peter 3:8-9).[105]

> We have different gifts, according to the grace given us…If it is contributing to the needs of others, let him give generously *(Romans 12:6,8)*.

*G*enerous. Perhaps that's the best word for describing a person with the gift of giving. In the original Greek text, the word "give" means "to share a thing with anyone, or to impart." Once again Webster's dictionary gives us food for thought. There we read that to give is "to be the source, produce; supply; as, cows give milk." Cows cannot *not* give milk. That's their function.

The concept of giving is a bit foreign to the thinking in our culture today. A person gives by turning over possessions or control of something to another person with no strings attached. There is no cost to the recipient. There is no bartering. The gift is given freely. Givers also will look for ways to give without drawing attention to themselves. And they enjoy giving without the pressure of an appeal. Similarly, parents look for ways to give to their children without the children demanding, expecting, or using some ploy to get what they want.

Giving sets a wonderful example for children because it helps them gain an understanding of how God gives through their parents.[106]

Rejoice with those who rejoice; mourn with those
who mourn. Live in harmony with one another…Do
not repay anyone evil for evil. Be careful to do what is
right in the eyes of everybody. If it is possible, as far as
it depends on you, live at peace with everyone. Do not
take revenge…"If your enemy is hungry, feed him; if he
is thirsty, give him something to drink. In doing this, you
will heap burning coals on his head" *(Romans 12:15-20)*.

❧

If every family lived this out in their daily interactions,
what a difference it would make! There are four guidelines here to make your life different. First, *empathize*
with your family members. Don't pop their balloon when
they're happy or joke around with them when they are
sad. The second guideline is to *relate* to everyone in the
family as well as their friends. Third, *don't try to get back
at someone* who hurts you. Let that person's comments
or actions slide by. After all, if you retaliate, you become
like that person. Is that what you want? Finally, surprise
those who hurt you by giving a gift. *Be generous. Be kind.
Be different.* And you and others will be blessed.[107]

In the LORD I take refuge. How then can you say to
me: "Flee like a bird to your mountain. For look, the
wicked bend their bows; they set their arrows against
the strings to shoot from the shadows at the upright in
heart. When the foundations are being destroyed, what
can the righteous do?" The LORD is in his holy temple;
the LORD is on his heavenly throne. He observes the
sons of men; his eyes examine them *(Psalm 11:1-4)*.

✦

"I'm fed up with this neighborhood—the schools, the
crime, the smog, the noise, the traffic—I'm out of here."
Millions of Americans move each year for a number of reasons. Some reasons are quite legitimate. Some people move
up, some down, some away, and some move only in their
minds. It's easy to get fed up with where we are and want
a better place. But just because we move to a new environment doesn't mean we'll necessarily experience a difference
in our lives. We may move to a different location, but all
too often we take our issues and problems with us.

David, the writer of today's verses, seems to be talking to many of us today. He reminds us that God still
rules. Perhaps we need to focus on that more than how
bad circumstances are around us.[108] Dean Merrill suggests that "the cure for our frustrations is not out there
somewhere. It is in the character of God, who loves us
and instills within us the fortitude to stand when life
appears to be collapsing."[109]

[There is] a time to be born and a time to die, a time to plant and a time to uproot *(Ecclesiastes 3:2)*.

Just wait. Someday it will arrive—the empty nest. Some parents can't wait for it, others dread it. For some couples, the empty nest is a major loss. It can bring on a mixture of different feelings as expressed in Ecclesiastes 3:1-8: weeping, laughing, mourning, healing, loving, releasing, losing, and relief. The atmosphere of the home changes. There are fewer choices to make, and there is less confusion and noise.

If a couple has relied upon the children to hold their relationship together or to preoccupy them, the last child's departure will create an enormous loss within the marital relationship. If a woman's only role is that of a mother, the leaving of the last child is accompanied by the removal of her identity. Such a situation may also reveal that intimacy has been absent in the marriage for many years, for the camouflage is no longer there. The empty nest also affects fathers. A child who was mother's little girl at age six may have become dad's special pal. When she leaves, he too could feel devastated.

What will it be like for you? It's not too early to think and talk about it.[110]

Without faith it is impossible to please God,
because anyone who comes to him must
believe that he exists and that he rewards those
who earnestly seek him *(Hebrews 11:6)*.

❧

According to the *Oxford Unabridged Dictionary*, the original meaning of the word *worry* was "to kill a person or animal by compressing the throat; to strangle or choke." Today *worry* is the fear of what might or might not happen. Is it wrong to worry?

Worry erodes our faith. God promises: "Do not fear, for I am with you; do not be dismayed, for I am your God. I will strengthen you and help you; I will uphold you" (Isaiah 41:10). What is Scripture saying?

- *Don't fear.* Why? Because God is with you.
- *Don't be dismayed.* Why? Because God will strengthen you, help you, and uphold you.

Did you know that *dismayed* is a word used to describe someone who looks around in bewilderment? Look what God does. He strengthens us. Strengthen means "to be alert or fortified." The word *help* in biblical Greek means "to surround." You'll be protected on all sides. Finally, *uphold* means "to sustain." So with all of what God has said He'll do, why worry?[111]

Better the little that the righteous have than the wealth
of many wicked...The days of the blameless are known
to the LORD, and their inheritance will endure forever.
In times of disaster they will not wither; in days of
famine they will enjoy plenty...I was young and now
I am old, yet I have never seen the righteous forsaken
or their children begging bread *(Psalm 37:16,18-19,25).*

Parenting, among other things, is *an act of financial faith.* If you were plotting your next 20 years with an eye to accumulate as much money as possible, you would never have kids. Kids are expensive—at least $100,000 apiece by the time you get them launched into adulthood and paying their own way. So if you take up the task of raising one or more children in North America today, you need today's verses!

God called us to be *parents.* And His call includes the promises that He will care for us; that He will guide our steps.[112]

Speaking the truth in love, we will in all things grow up
into him who is the Head, that is, Christ *(Ephesians 4:15)*.

J ust live and let live" is a motto many people live by. They
say, "Let everyone be who they are the way they are.
If you really love people you won't try to change them."
Generally that perspective isn't so bad. We do need to
respect the God-given uniqueness the Lord has built into
each of us. However, you don't have to read much of the
Bible to realize that one of God's primary goals for us as
Christians is that we *grow*.

While God loves us just the way we are, He also loves
us too much to leave us that way. Our willingness to
change, to learn, to grow is God's love language. It tells
Him we believe in Him, we trust Him, and we want to
be who and what He wants us to be. Openness to change
is our way of taking His hand and following Him.

Israel loved Joseph more than any of his other
sons, because he had been born to him in his
old age; and he made a richly ornamented robe
for him. When his brothers saw that their father
loved him more than any of them, they hated him
and could not speak a kind word to him. Joseph
had a dream, and when he told it to his brothers,
they hated him all the more *(Genesis 37:3-5)*.

Partiality. Favoritism. Think back to when you were a
child. Wasn't there another child who was a favorite—
someone who seemed to get more attention than you and
the other kids? Perhaps it was someone in your family or
school or some group. Perhaps it was someone you didn't
like. Or a friend, a sibling, or…even you.

Think about your family. Are there any favorites? Who
might be neglected? Ask God to help all of you balance
the attention and love in your family. Remember to thank
God that He doesn't play favorites. "God does not show
favoritism" (Romans 2:11).

Here is my servant whom I have chosen, the
one I love, in whom I delight *(Matthew 12:18)*.

❧

When we signed on to become parents, we probably didn't realize our job description included
becoming servants. Some positions of serving are recognized and appreciated. In others we feel taken for granted.
Unfortunately, we live in a world that doesn't value the
servant role. We'd rather get than give, take than share,
and grasp than release. Children reflect this tendency.
We have to teach them to be other-centered. It's all too
natural to be self-centered.

Perhaps we're all afraid of what being a servant might
cost us. There are risks. We can focus on the risks involved
or we can focus on service as a privilege and a learning
experience.[113] "If Christ, Lord of the universe, became a
Servant for us, can we do any less for Him?"[114]

How can each person in your family be more of a servant today? Take a few moments to discuss that now.

Remember the sabbath day, to keep
it holy *(Exodus 20:8 NASB)*.

⤳

Busy, busy, busy. Does that sound familiar? Especially if you have children. Sometimes parents say, "I've got so much going on and so much to do that I don't even remember what it's like to slow down, let alone stop!" Have you ever had days when you're on the go from dawn to dusk and the only reason you collapse on the bed is because you simply ran out of gas? All parents experience that from time to time. Sometimes the frantic pace is within the home. Other times it's outside the home.

It used to be that people looked forward to Sunday as their day of rest and worship. But when was the last time Sunday was a day of rest and worship for you? Sometimes we make Sundays a catch-up day for the leftovers from the week. Soon Sunday blends together with the other days.

Why don't you try to do something different this Sunday? Worship—really worship—and then rest.

As a father has compassion on his children, so the LORD has compassion on those who fear him *(Psalm 103:13)*.

⌇

Do you ever feel like some of your concerns are too insignificant to bother God with? Perhaps you've looked at the work that's piling up, the kids who need to be chauffeured, and the car that needs a new transmission, and you've wondered if God cares about these kinds of details.

Do *children* wonder if God cares about the little things? It doesn't appear so. Listen to their prayers. They're usually simple, basic, trusting, and they include everything from the new pet rabbit to another child liking them at school.

But still we can't help but wonder if God notices—especially if we're taken for granted by other family members. If no one shows any concern about how hard you work to make a living, why would God be concerned? Well, take heart. God is a God of compassion, and He's concerned about everything. There are no limits. He is a gentle, caring father.

Make my joy complete by being like-
minded, having the same love, being one
in spirit and purpose *(Philippians 2:2)*.

Most Christian parents would do the right thing if they were sure what the right thing was. But what does a good parent do? Should you try to control your children? Is loving them the same as controlling them? Is controlling them the same as disciplining them?

> The two most powerful influences in parent-
> ing are control and support. Parental control
> is defined as the ability to manage a child's
> behavior. Parental support is defined as the
> ability to make a child feel loved...
> The best children come from parents who
> can manage their behavior and communicate
> their unconditional love. The worst children
> come from homes where they are controlled
> but not loved. You may not be able to manage
> your child's behavior, but by the grace of God
> you can love him.[115]

That is the way God loves us. He doesn't try to domi-
nate our lives, but draws us to Him through His love.

The people complained about their hardships
in the hearing of the LORD *(Numbers 11:1).*

Don't grumble against each other, brothers, or you will
be judged. The Judge is standing at the door! *(James 5:9).*

❦

Gripe, gripe, gripe. Complain, complain, complain.
Some of us are like that. There are some homes
where griping and complaining are the norm and cheerfulness is the exception. These homes are anything but
healthy. The atmosphere in them breeds pessimism, bitterness, and gloom.

What can you do to avoid this? Begin each day by
finding three reasons to praise and thank the Lord. Write
them down, and read your list several times a day. Make
a pact with your family that the first four minutes of the
morning when you first see everyone and the first four
minutes when people come home you will be positive,
affirming, and affectionate. By making such a commitment for these key times, you will help set the mood for
the day and the evening.

Come to me, all you who are weary and burdened,
and I will give you rest *(Matthew 11:28)*.

❧

New babies are miracles. But along with their presence in your life comes another new resident—weariness. The following prayer for a new mother and her trying circumstances can be adapted by you to fit your situation in life. Reflect on this prayer—or your version of it—when you're weary.

> O Lord, help me…
> I love this little child,
> but I am physically and emotionally worn out.
> Infants are demanding—late nights,
> daybreak mornings,
> unpredictable schedules.
> I keep waiting for things to get back to
>   normal,
> only to realize this is now normal…
> Calm me, Lord…Help me relax as I realize
> an infant is more than smiles, rosy cheeks,
> and affectionate sounds.
> But a child, a new baby, is a miracle—
> new, ongoing life in your creation…[116]

God created man in his own image *(Genesis 1:27)*.

❧

A baby is born. There's joy and delight…then specula-
tion. Who does he or she look like? The eyes, the
nose, the legs…the older a child becomes, the more he
or she begins to resemble someone. We all want our children to resemble us in some way. Some children have been
told they resemble their grandfather, uncle, or someone
else. Some adopted children have been told they look
just like their parents! These resemblances are not just
physical qualities.

The image that all of us have as believers is Jesus.
That's who we resemble. Dr. Larry Crabb, in his book
Understanding People, suggested several ways we resem-
ble God:

- We, like our heavenly Father, have a longing for close relationships.

- We were born with a desire to be close to
  God and people.

- We…experience free will. God does what
  He wants and so do we.

- Like God we experience emotions.

- Finally, like God, we are spiritual beings.

Who do you resemble?[117]

Pray continually *(1 Thessalonians 5:17)*.

~~~

Many parents are now personalizing Scripture to create specific prayers for their children. The following are prayers based upon Scripture.

Courage

I pray that when my child passes through the water You will be there and through the rivers, that my child will not be overflowed by them. When my child walks through the fire, that there will be no burning nor scorching. For You are the Lord God (see Isaiah 43:2-3).

Faith

I pray that my child will walk by faith and not by sight (see 2 Corinthians 5:7).

Salvation

I pray, Lord Jesus, that my child will come to understand what You meant when You said, "Whoever confesses Me before men, him I will also confess before My Father who is in heaven" (see Matthew 10:32).

You can create other prayers by using a topical index of the Scriptures. Use your children's names when you pray and discover the benefits and joy of praying God's Word for your children.[118]

Blessed is he whose help is the God of Jacob,
whose hope is in the LORD his God *(Psalm 146:5)*.

⌒

Did you know that happiness is biblical? It is—but
Scripture often uses the word *blessed* because the
Greek word literally means both "happy" and "blessed."
In the beatitudes, for example, you could just as well sub-
stitute the word *happy* for blessed.

Blessed does have a unique and special meaning. It tells
us that the happiness God gives is special. It's because
of how He has blessed us that we can be happy. But is
happiness the same as joy? No, there is a distinction. The
word for *joy* is found in both Matthew and Luke, and
it can mean "joy" or "delight." The source of that joy is
our life in Christ.

Do your children see joy in your life? Do they see
you happy? Do you see joy in their lives? *Lasting* joy? At
the next meal or ride in the car, why don't all of you talk
about joy and pray for it. God is waiting to help you discover joy.[119]

From everlasting to everlasting the LORD's love is
with those who fear him, and his righteousness
with their children's children *(Psalm 103:17)*.

~~~

Let's imagine for a moment that you're having a conversation with God. He is going to respond to you in
an audible voice with very specific instructions.

Dear Parent,

More than anything I want to see My Son
Jesus Christ formed in your children (Galatians 4:19). I desire that your children will be
taught about Me so that they will know great
peace (Isaiah 54:13). I want your children to
train themselves to distinguish between good
and evil as well as develop a healthy conscience
(Hebrews 5:14; 1 Peter 3:21). It's also important
for them to put My law into their minds and
on their hearts (Hebrews 8:10).

It's important that you help your children
choose friends who are wise…I want them to
remain sexually pure and always call upon Me
and My grace to help them keep this commitment (Ephesians 5:3,31-33). I believe you will
appreciate My last desire, which Paul mentioned in Ephesians 6:1-2: I want them to honor
you at all times.

I am here to help you. Remember the extent
of My love for you.

How much more will your Father in heaven give
good gifts to those who ask him! *(Matthew 7:11).*

❧

D id you know that your own father has affected the
way you perceive God?

If your father was patient, you are more likely
to see God as patient and available for you.
You feel that you are worth God's time and
concern. You feel important to God and that
He is personally involved in every aspect of
your life.

If your father was kind, you probably see
God acting kindly and graciously on your
behalf. You feel that you are worth God's help
and intervention. You feel God's love for you
deeply and you're convinced that He wants to
relate to you personally.

If your father was a giving man, you may
perceive God as someone who gives to you
and supports you. You feel that you are worth
God's support and encouragement.[120]

Accurate beliefs about God are based on His Word.
Knowing who He is and what He is like will help all
of us become the parents we want to be and that God
wants us to be!

Be subject to one another in the fear
of Christ *(Ephesians 5:21 NASB)*.

～

To a Child About to Be Married

When you marry, you are giving up your single life and taking on the biblical role of a servant to the person you love. To put it simply, your role is to make sure your partner's needs are met. In a marriage relationship, being a servant is an act of love, a gift to your partner to make his or her life fuller. It is an act of strength and not of weakness. It is a positive action that has been chosen to show your love to each other.

A servant may also be called an "enabler," in the good sense of the word, which means "to make better." As an enabler you are to make life easier for your partner instead of placing restrictive demands upon him or her.

A servant is also someone who edifies another person. First Corinthians 8:1 sums up the matter of edifying: "Love builds up." That is your calling—never tear down, don't just maintain, but always build up.

Call to me and I will answer you and tell you great and
unsearchable things you do not know *(Jeremiah 33:3).*

❧

"C an't be done. Tried it. Just won't work. Nope, it's
impossible." Words and phrases such as these bring
progress to a roaring halt and deaden the creativity of
people around us. Sometimes we adults rely so much
on our years of experience and knowledge that we stifle
the learning experiences of our children by failing to let
them learn on their own. Some of us seem to have the
gift of throwing in the towel. It may be we feel it's a waste
of time to try something new. But what would happen
if we eliminated those words from our vocabulary and
were willing to say, "Let's give it a try"?

What have you been seeing as impossible in your life?
In your children's lives? Have you ever heard the phrase,
"The impossible is the untried"? *Impossible* isn't a word God
ever uses or calls us to use. Instead, He says the opposite:
Try it. Go for it. Let's do it together![121]

You shall have no other gods before me *(Exodus 20:3)*.

❧

Competition is a part of our lives whether we want it or not. The networks on television compete to capture your attention. They want to be first in the ratings. Family members have been known to compete against each other. Who hasn't heard of sibling rivalry? Your children probably compete for your attention. The things most important to us are usually those items we strive for. In a sense, they become number one to us, and we don't want anything to keep us from having them.

All the delights of your life and what you value most need a slight adjustment. They need to be moved to second place in your life. Once you became a Christian, it's as though you have a parking lot and there's a space reserved for the owner. It's *the* most important spot. It has easy access. God is your owner now. First place is reserved for Him. Not your children, your spouse, your career, your money, your house, but God.

I am fearfully and wonderfully made *(Psalm 139:14).*

E motions—feelings—those elusive responses that avoid predictability. Why do they cause us so much trouble? Who needs them? Where did they come from? There's a simple answer. They're a gift…from God. He created you and your children with emotions. Sometimes you may think somebody got an extra dose!

If our children are going to have a solid foundation for their emotional expressions later in life, they need to be encouraged to both experience and express a wide range of emotions. That means their emotional experiences must not be limited to pleasant emotions. If they are only allowed to experience one side of their emotions, they will have a limited awareness of who they are and a distorted perspective of others. Children should not only be allowed, but enthusiastically encouraged, to experience happiness and sadness, hope and fear, joy and depression, jealousy and compassion.

Perhaps the best way is for them to see a healthy display of emotions in their parents. There are benefits for both you and them.

Do not conform any longer to the pattern
of this world, but be transformed by the
renewing of your mind (*Romans 12:2*).

❧

Christians are people who are called to be exceptions. We are to be different and stand apart from society. Christian parents want their children to be exceptions as well. Usually they want them to do and be the best they can to the fullest of their abilities. But what's most important is character. What better schooling can children have than to see their parents exhibit good character qualities? Consider the following qualities for yourself first, and then as positive goals for your children's lives.

- If we're not going to be conformed to this world, we need to be people of *integrity*.

- *Credibility* does tie into performance. It's earned by constantly doing the best, being faithful, and following through.

- *Responsibility* is a trait we would all love to see in our children.

- Right along with this is *dependability*— follow-through.

How are these four character qualities reflected in day-to-day events by each family member? Think about it. Pray about it. Talk about it.[122]

"In your anger do not sin": Do not let the sun go down while you are still angry *(Ephesians 4:26)*.

❧

We all want peaceful children. Dr. Archibald Hart suggests several ways to make this a reality.

1. *Teach your child to deal with each hurt as it arises.* Accumulated hurts seem overwhelming.

2. *Teach your child to take responsibility for his or her anger.* No one "makes" him or her angry.

3. *Teach your child to allow other people to have feelings.* Anger is seldom one-sided. Others have a right to feel angry also.

4. *Listen, receive, and accept your child's anger.* Talking about anger helps pinpoint its source and may diffuse its intensity.

5. *Show your child how to forgive.* Explain why revenge is dangerous.

6. *Teach your child to seek reconciliation.* Reconciliation restores broken relationships. If your child can forgive and be reconciled to those who cause hurt, he or she will have no problem dealing with life's hurts.[123]

That's good advice for adults too!

"Do you hear what these children are saying?"
they asked him. "Yes," replied Jesus, "have you
never read, 'From the lips of children and infants
you have ordained praise'?" *(Matthew 21:16).*

~~≈~~

Television and newspapers regularly tell us about parents who save their children from some disaster. Now and then, however, we hear just the reverse. The parents were saved by a child:

> A three-year-old son of a Maplewood, Missouri police officer told his father, "You forgot this" and handed him his bulletproof vest as he was leaving to go on duty. The father probably chuckled about it at first, but later on when a burglar shot him in the chest, he was thankful for his child saving his life.

What have you learned from your child? What could you learn from your child? What might you need to learn from your child? Talk about these questions as a family. Your child has something to teach you. Are you willing to listen?[124]

Pray continually *(1 Thessalonians 5:17)*.

⌇

Each day brings with it a multitude of possibilities as well as problems. What a difference it makes when we begin the day by communicating with our heavenly Father and continue this throughout the day. Praying in their own words for their needs as well as using guided prayer from the pens of others is a practice many people engage in from time to time. Voice aloud this prayer by an unknown author:

> Thank You, God, for this new day,
>   for the life You are giving each member
>   of my family:
> Thank You for blessing each one of us
>   with the strength and health we need
>   to serve you today,
>   with the joy we need not to give in to
>   discouragement, anger, or boredom,
>   with the protection we need against
>   physical and moral danger,
>   with the love we need to give hope to
>   those we meet.

He himself is our peace, who has made the
two one and has destroyed the barrier, the
dividing wall of hostility *(Ephesians 2:14).*

—⊱⊰—

Fatigue, weariness, exhaustion. These seem to be the
built-in companions of parenthood. In fact, whenever
a baby is born it seems to bring these companions into
the home as uninvited guests. Every parent feels completely worn out at one time or another. That's normal.
You're not going to feel at the end of a day like you did
in the morning.

Some days you may want to wave a white flag of surrender. Some days you may get weary of waiting. Weariness
is a sign that you need to rest and refresh. If you don't,
you could move easily into the malady called burnout.
Yes, there is such a thing as parental burnout! And you
don't recover very quickly from it.

God's Word can refresh you. Stop several times a day,
quit giving, and start receiving. Take in His Word. Let it
refresh you. Why not take a minute to look up and read
Isaiah 40:28-31? You'll be glad you did!

Discipline your son, for in that there is hope; do not
be a willing party to his death *(Proverbs 19:18)*.

~~~

Frustration, chaos, exhaustion—the three plagues of parenthood. They often seep into our lives when we're trying to control our children. Sometimes our children can act like they are deaf and dumb—at least toward us. What can you do to get a child to respond?

You could make a request. A request is a question with a directive in it. It's a question in which we have a prescribed answer that we want. Or as one parent said, "I'd better get it or else!" But a request, in a proper tone of voice, lets a child know that we believe he or she can do what we are asking and that we respect his or her opinion and are willing to consider some alternatives. A request can also point toward the behavior or response we want instead of reinforcing what the child might have been doing wrong. Requests are the most positive options.

But if it doesn't work, why keep on doing it? Be creative. Be resourceful. Be prayerful. And you will find a way that works.

The crowds answered, "This is Jesus, the prophet
from Nazareth in Galilee" *(Matthew 21:11)*.

~~⌇~~

I f someone claimed to be a prophet today, people would
laugh. But this title given to Jesus was the highest compliment that could be given to someone in His day.

There were many prophets in Israel during Old Testament times. These men were chosen by God to reveal
something about the future or pass along a message.

> *Isaiah* taught about God's holiness and
> shared about the coming Messiah.
>
> *Jeremiah* taught the people about the impor-
> tance of their own personal faith.
>
> *Ezekiel,* in his unique way, described God's
> special relationship with Israel.
>
> *Daniel* clarified God's sovereignty.
>
> *Hosea* emphasized God's love for sinners.

Then came another prophet—Jesus. He was different.
Paul Harvey, a noted newscaster for many years, ended
his descriptive stories with the phrase "And that's the rest
of the story." That's what Jesus was: the rest of the story.
He was the prophet who brought it all together and gave
a full disclosure of God.[125]

Give to the Lord the glory due to His name;
worship the Lord *(Psalm 29:2 AMP)*.

L oss has been mentioned in the pages of this devotional. There's a reason for that. Sometimes life seems
as though we are going from one loss to another. The more
people there are in your family unit, the more potential
there is for loss.

There are numerous ways to handle the losses of life.
One of them is worship. Yes, worship. Richard Exley
explains:

> We don't worship God because of our losses,
> but in spite of them. We don't praise Him
> for the tragedies, but in them. Like Job, we
> hear God speak to us out of the storm (Job
> 38:1). Like the disciples at sea in a small boat,
> caught in a severe storm, we too see Jesus
> coming to us in the fourth watch of the
> night. We hear Him say, "Take courage! It
> is I. Don't be afraid" (Matthew 14:27).[126]

You see, in worship the focus is on God. And that
in itself can give us the resources we need to handle the
difficulties of life.

Whoever exalts himself will be humbled, and whoever
humbles himself will be exalted *(Matthew 23:12)*.

❧

I t's a case of the swelled head, the inflated ego, the over-
impressed view of oneself. And whatever swells up or
inflates is often popped! You've probably overinflated a
balloon and seen it stretch and strain until there's no
room left for any more air.

When we surround ourselves with mirrors the only
reflection we see is that of ourselves. Remember the mirrors in the old fun houses? They distorted our images
and made us look huge or grotesque. That's the way it is
with pride. It's an unduly high and exaggerated opinion
of oneself. More specifically, pride is conceit.

When you see pride in your children, you want to
shake it right out of them because it has such a negative
effect on life and friendships. But pride affects something
else too, according to Dr. Lloyd Ogilvie:

- Pride takes the place of praise in our
  hearts.

- Pride pollutes everything it touches.

- Spiritual pride is the root of all other
  manifestations of pride. It is Satan's most
  powerful tool. With it we can miss meeting the Lord.[127]

Now to Him who is able to do far more
abundantly beyond all that we ask or think,
according to the power that works within us,
to Him be glory *(Ephesians 3:20-21 NASB)*.

~~~

I t's fascinating to watch eagles soar. Perhaps you've had
the opportunity to see them in the wild. They take
off from their perches and use the tremendous power of
their wings to gain the height they need. When they hit
the fast-moving air currents, they quit flapping, spread
their wings, and allow the air currents to help them soar.
God created these creatures in a marvelous, sensitive way.
It's not easy to soar!

You and I have been given a power through Jesus Christ
to stabilize our lives. We're constantly confronted with
turbulence. When we allow Jesus Christ to control our
imagination, our thought lives, and our wills, we then
have the power we need to soar. Ask Him today to use
your imagination to envision what you never dreamed
possible. Commit your will to Him for decisions you
need to make.[128]

Wait for the LORD; be strong and take heart
and wait for the LORD *(Psalm 27:14)*.

～≫⊱～

Have you ever ached over the disappointment experienced by your child? Parents do that. There is some upsetting event, loss, or even tragedy in your child's life. You wish he or she didn't have to experience that, and you wish you could take it all away. Literally your heart and the rest of you aches for him or her. Many times you can't make the situation different for either one of you. You and your child can find comfort by focusing on God's Word:

> May integrity and uprightness protect me, because my hope is in you (Psalm 25:21).

> Be still before the LORD and wait patiently for him; do not fret when men succeed in their ways, when they carry out their wicked schemes (Psalm 37:7).

> If any of you lacks wisdom, he should ask God, who gives generously to all without finding fault, and it will be given to him (James 1:5).

Just as you received Christ Jesus as Lord, continue
to live in him, rooted and built up in him,
strengthened in the faith as you were taught, and
overflowing with thankfulness *(Colossians 2:6-7)*.

I n school, our children take exams and quizzes. Here's
an exam for you.

- I would be more successful if…
- I would be more significant if…
- I would be more fulfilled if…
- I would be more satisfied if…
- I would be happier if…
- I would be more secure if…
- I would have more peace if…

How you finish these statements reflects your present
belief system. That's right—this quiz is a window into
the beliefs that are important to you. Why not have your
family do this too…and discuss the results.[129]

A bruised reed he will not break, and a
smoldering wick he will not snuff out, till he
leads justice to victory *(Matthew 12:20)*.

One of the vital elements of a candle is the wick. Without a wick, it couldn't perform its function. The wick holds the fire and burns slowly so the wax can melt gradually. After many hours, when the wax is almost gone and the wick has burned away, the candlelight begins to flicker. The flame is on the verge of going out.

As a parent, you may have days when the way you feel is best described by the candle. You may feel as though your wick is smoldering just on the verge of going out. You don't want it to, but you can't stop the wax from melting around you. That's when you want to listen to God. Not only does He say He will not put out a weak flame, but He also is available for you at such a time as this. Wick extensions are available! Ask, believe, and receive.

My guilt has overwhelmed me like a
burden too heavy to bear *(Psalm 38:4)*.

There it is again—a twinge—that little irritating feeling
that speaks volumes. You know what it is: guilt. It's a
feeling of remorse over wrong words or actions or a sense
of regret because you failed to speak up or do something
when it was needed. You'd like to go back and change
what you did, but you can't. Neither can you evict that
unwelcome tenant called guilt.

God knows about guilt. Often we experience it because
we have done something against Him. There's a positive
side to the guilt felt by you and your children. Guilt tells
you when you've done something wrong. But you don't
want to wallow in it. Take the next step and follow God's
plan: "If we confess our sins, he is faithful and just and
will forgive us our sins and purify us from all unrighteousness" (1 John 1:9). When you accept this wonderful
gift called *grace,* the mantle of guilt you've been wearing turns to dust.

His mouth is sweetness itself; he is altogether lovely.
This is my lover, this my friend *(Song of Songs 5:16)*.

~

There are many dimensions of love in marriage. One of the most important is friendship. What does friendship love entail? It's an unselfish dedication to your partner's happiness. It's when the fulfillment of his or her needs becomes one of your needs. It's learning to enjoy what your partner enjoys.

Your friendship will mean you can enjoy some aspects of life together, but you're also comfortable with having your own individual interests.

Friendship love also involves a certain level of intimacy in which there is openness, vulnerability, and emotional connection. Never become a stranger to your partner in any area of life.

Remember that marriages that last are marriages that have a husband and wife who are friends. As your friendship develops over the years, you will find that you choose each other for just the joy of the other person's company. Be sure to practice your friendship. Friendship is part of God's intention for marriage.

Carry each other's burdens, and in this way you
will fulfill the law of Christ *(Galatians 6:2)*.

⤙⤚

Life can be filled with tough times. If you complete your years of parenting without experiencing some type of family crisis or loss, you'll be the exception. Some families handle difficulties well and survive. Others are totally disrupted, and some even disintegrate.

What do families do who make it through their crises? First, *they don't allow themselves to become bitter.* They refuse to live in the past or permit the situation to bring life to a stop.

Second, *they live in the present and have a future perspective.* They seek to learn from what has happened and don't wallow in regrets. They also learn to view the future as an opportunity.

Third, *they learn to manage and resolve their conflicts.* Families that don't do this heap one conflict upon another. And when a new one comes, they respond to it out of the contamination of all the unresolved issues.

Where does your family fit in these characteristics? How are you handling crises? What you learn now will help you in the future.

Do not conform any longer to the pattern
of this world, but be transformed by the
renewing of your mind *(Romans 12:2)*.

✋

"I just don't fit in. I hate that new school. Everyone is so different. I'm the odd one." These are the laments of a child. But adults experience the same feelings too. We struggle with possessiveness, cliques at church, jealousy in the office, and favoritism in the higher echelons of the company and wonder, *How can I fit in?*

To fit in, many people compromise, especially in their teens and twenties. In the workplace some people compromise their values to gain a promotion and status. You may be able to fit in, but first evaluate the cost. Why is it so important to you? Do you really need what you're working so hard to achieve?

We've actually been called to be aliens in this world—to be different and *not* fit in. Have you ever given yourself permission not to fit into a certain situation? Proclaim that you don't fit in and rejoice over it! Experience your newfound freedom.

By the grace given me I say to every one of you: Do not think of yourself more highly than you ought, but rather think of yourself with sober judgment *(Romans 12:3)*.

※

Here is a brief quiz: Who is the most important person in your family? Naturally, the Lord is—that's obvious. But let's consider all the other members of your household: parents, children, even your pet dog or cat. Now, who is the most important and why? What about the one who...

- makes the money to pay bills?
- is the most responsive to meeting the needs of other family members?
- oversees everyone else to make sure they don't forget anything and are on time?
- brings the most joy and laughter into the house?
- has the greatest potential for the future?

Those are some choices, aren't they? We all feel at times that we contribute the most and that the family couldn't get along without us. But no doubt the other family members feel the same way about themselves! So who's the most important? You are. They are. You all are.[130]

Fathers, do not irritate and provoke your children to anger [do not exasperate them to resentment], but rear them [tenderly] in the training and discipline and the counsel and admonition of the Lord *(Ephesians 6:4 AMP)*.

~⊱~

It's all too easy for children to find their identities wrapped up in performance and appearance. Why? Largely because those are the values their parents and teachers reinforce. Children are applauded if they're cute, if they get straight A's, if they say funny jokes, or if they hit home runs.

But what about the child who isn't cute or entertaining? What about the child who never wins a starring role in the school play or strikes out most of the time in baseball? What if your child is below average academically? Tragically, children like these are often compared, rejected, and ignored by the adults in their lives—including their own parents! So the children begin to question their identities and doubt their worth. The false values our society promotes can even pervade our Christian homes.

What about you? Do you struggle with identity and self-acceptance issues?[131]

My son, keep your father's commands and do not
forsake your mother's teaching *(Proverbs 6:20)*.

~

Parents are told, "Someday your children will move out.
They'll be on their own, and you'll have to let them
go." That's true, but letting go is not a one-time act; it's
an ongoing process throughout their lifetimes. But what
does letting go mean on a daily basis? Chuck Swindoll
describes it best:

> To let go doesn't mean to stop caring,
>   it means I can't do it for someone else.
> To let go is not to cut myself off,
>   it's the realization that I can't control another.
> To let go is not to enable,
>   but to allow learning from natural consequences.
> To let go is to admit powerlessness,
>   which means the outcome is not in my hands.
> To let go is not to try to change or blame another,
>   I can only change myself.
> To let go is not to care for,
>   but to care about.
> To let go is not to fix,
>   but to be supportive.
> To let go is not to judge,
>   but to allow another to be a human being.[132]

Isn't this the carpenter? *(Mark 6:3).*

M ost of us don't spend much time thinking about Jesus as a carpenter. It doesn't seem so significant. And yet, maybe it does at that. A carpenter is someone who fashions and creates. Jesus did this both in the expression of His divinity and His humanity. He created the universe. But He also fashioned simple pieces of furniture for people.

If anyone knew about hard, arduous work it was Jesus. He didn't have a "Home Improvement" set with drills and electric saws. He had rough tools that were very basic and required muscle power and produced calluses. His hands were probably covered with numerous bruises and cuts that came from handling wood and His crude tools. You wouldn't believe the amount of time and energy it probably took to make a simple chair or table.

All your effort and toil as a parent has purpose and merit even though you wonder at times if it's worth it. As Jesus is fashioning your life, let Him work through you to fashion your child's life.

Finally, brothers, whatever is true, whatever is noble, whatever is right, whatever is pure, whatever is lovely, whatever is admirable—if anything is excellent or praiseworthy—think about such things *(Philippians 4:8).*

꿀

Children are afraid of monsters, but they also like them. They are usually fascinated by them, read about them, watch them on television, and use them to scare other children. But monsters are just for kids, right? Well, maybe not.

What's your dream? Is it a dream…or more of a nightmare? Some adults do live with monsters pursuing them—in their minds. Sometimes our dreams become portrayals of our thoughts. We give our thoughts and fantasies free rein and the monsters in our minds put on a cloak of reality.

Is there any monster in your life that has been given room to roam? If so, remember that monsters can be tamed! They're only as powerful as our thoughts, and God's Word tells us what to do with those—think on whatever is true. For adults, monsters aren't fun. Just remember: What your monster does is up to you. It's your dream![133]

The joy of the LORD is your strength *(Nehemiah 8:10).*

❧

Mothers and fathers need strength. Lots of it. Your exhaustion will come from too little time for too much to do, restless nights, demands unmatched with your resources, and sudden traumatic events that no one could possibly ever prepare for.

There is a well that never runs dry and will give you the strength of heart and mind you need. When one of "those days" hits and you feel like you're trying to guide a plow through rocky ground with no one around to help shoulder the load, go to the Scripture. Stop, sit down, take a breath, and read. Silently or out loud. Let the words soak through and saturate you.

> The LORD is my rock, my fortress and my deliverer; my God is my rock, in whom I take refuge. He is my shield and the horn of my salvation, my stronghold (Psalm 18:2).

> The LORD is my light and my salvation—whom shall I fear? (Psalm 27:1).

Fathers, do not provoke or irritate or fret your
children [do not be hard on them or harass
them], lest they become discouraged and sullen
and morose and feel inferior and frustrated. [Do
not break their spirit] *(Colossians 3:21 AMP).*

That's good enough."

"That's not good enough."

You probably heard these two comments as a child,
and you probably say them to yourself now. They're both
okay, especially the first one, when it comes to being a
parent.

Too many parents want to be perfect. Instead, they
end up feeling like failures, frustrated over their inability to attain the impossible. Perfectionistic parents also
are too demanding of their children. People who can't
accept themselves unless they're perfect won't accept the
efforts of other people.

But good-enough parents do what they can for the
benefit of children. They recognize what they can and
can't do and the strengths and limitations of their circumstances. Yes, they'll make mistakes. Everyone does.

Ease up on yourself, strengthen what needs to be
strengthened, be available and involved, and above all,
relax and enjoy your children.[134]

I pray that you may be active in sharing your faith,
so that you will have a full understanding of every
good thing we have in Christ…I do wish, brother,
that I may have some benefit from you in the
Lord; refresh my heart in Christ *(Philemon 6,20)*.

People joke around about our inability to take possessions with us into heaven. But who would want to?
What would you want to take for the duration of eternity
aside from your family?

Perhaps the question shouldn't be "What would you
like to take with you?" but "Who would you like to take?"
Who do you want to spend eternity with who doesn't
yet know Jesus as his or her Savior? That puts a whole
new light on the subject, doesn't it? Do you have a list of
people you're praying for so you all can spend eternity
together? That's a good place to begin. Once their names
are on a list, then your prayers for them can be more frequent and consistent.

God wants us to tell other people about the salvation
that we've been given.[135]

"In your anger do not sin": Do not let the sun go down while you are still angry (Ephesians 4:26).

❧

Every child gets angry. So does every parent. A child will yell, spit, swear, hold his breath, kick, scream—and you could probably add more expressions of anger. Anger is a natural response; it's a God-created emotion. Children are not born with control over their anger. They have to learn it. Some do, some don't. What can you do to help your children?

Teach your children the cause of their anger. Usually anger is a "secondary" emotion caused by fear, hurt, or frustration. Teach your children to ask themselves why they are angry. Let them talk about their anger in a constructive way. Help them accept the responsibility for their anger. Help your children choose how they are going to respond. Give them a choice.

And by the way, what do you do when you're angry?

There is a time for everything, and a season for
every activity under heaven *(Ecclesiastes 3:1).*

❧

L et's imagine that you've just received a sweepstakes
letter in the mail that says "Congratulations, parent.
You are a winner. Yes, a winner of $1,440! You can spend
the money for anything you want—but there's one stipu-
lation: You must spend it all within 24 hours. You can't
save it or give away any portion of it. It must be spent
by you."

What would you do with $1,440? If you're a saver you
might want to put it in your savings account, but the
letter says you can't do that. Nor can you share it with
your children. You must spend it! So...how will you use
it? But wait! Before you have any visions of a new couch
or golf clubs, the $1,440 you're being given isn't really
money...it's minutes.

You are given 1,440 minutes to spend during each
day of your life, and it can't be saved or given away. Are
you seizing each moment and getting the most out of it?
How are you using your daily allotment?[136]

Cast all your anxiety on him because
he cares for you *(1 Peter 5:7)*.

~≫

Nobody likes stress—that feeling of being pulled tight like an overstretched rubber band. An old Anglo-Saxon definition of the word was "to strangle or choke." Parents battle stress, and so do children. Sometimes parents feel helpless because they're not sure how to help their children learn to cope with stress. There are some basic steps you may already be taking, but it helps to be reminded. Here's what works: Children need parents who care deeply about them and who are available physically, emotionally, and spiritually.

Another help in overcoming stress is the availability of a caring and loving extended family or other adults.

It's also essential that children live in an abuse-free environment. Did you know that yelling is classified as emotional abuse? Perhaps we need to watch the volume of our voices more carefully in our homes.

Also, accept your child for whom he or she is. Children who like themselves and can accept their strengths and weaknesses have resilience.[137]

Trust in the L ORD with all your heart and lean not
on your own understanding *(Proverbs 3:5)*.

⤳

Dear God,

I am powerless and my life is unmanageable
without Your love and guidance.
I come to You today because I believe that
You can restore and renew me
to meet my needs tomorrow
and to help me meet the needs of my children.

Since I cannot manage my life or affairs,
I have decided to give them to You.
I put my life, my will, my thoughts,
my desires and ambitions in Your hands.
I give You each of my children.

I cannot control or change my children,
other family members or friends,
so I release them into Your care
for Your loving hands to do with as You will.
Just keep me loving and free from judging them.

If they need changing, God,
You'll have to do it; I can't.
Just make me willing and ready
to be of service to You,
to have my shortcomings removed,
and to do my best.[138]

"Come, follow me," Jesus said (*Matthew 4:19*).

❧

Why follow Jesus? Because everything He said and did was in our best interest.

Christ said to follow Him because following anyone or anything else gets us lost.

Christ said to know who we look like because drawing our self-image from any other source but God poisons our souls and spirits.

Christ said to love our neighbor as ourselves because we grow the most when committed to fostering another's growth, not just our own…

Christ said to get real because wearing masks makes our lives empty and our relationships unfulfilling.

Christ said to stop blaming others because taking responsibility for our own problems is essential for true maturity and health.

Christ said to forgive others because unforgiveness is arrogant and hurts others as well as ourselves…

Everything Christ tells us is in our best interest, and it is critically important to understand that. His counsel wasn't designed to burden us, but to set us free. When He gave His counsel to us, it was aimed at meeting our deepest needs and it will if we follow it.[139]

Your hands made me and fashioned
me *(Psalm 119:73 NASB).*

⤳

Emotions! Who needs them? All of us do. Our emotions influence almost every aspect of our lives. And God speaks to us through our emotions.

Sin has led us to respond to our emotions in one of two unhealthy ways. First, we can deny or ignore them. Unfortunately, when we ignore or minimize the emotional realities of our lives we distort our perspectives, limit our perceptions, and lead ourselves to distrust our experiences. Second, we can allow ourselves to be controlled by our emotions. This is equally dangerous.

Whether you deny or ignore your emotions (option #1) or you embrace them and ignore your intellect (option #2), your response is not healthy.

By God's grace, there is a third option. The healthy response is to view our emotions from God's perspective and to bring them into harmony with our minds. Maturity involves the whole person. It is impossible to be spiritually mature and emotionally immature. True maturity involves bringing balance to our heart, head, and will—to our feelings, thoughts, and actions. Each aspect of our lives is important. Each was designed by God for our good. Each is a manifestation of the image of God in us.[140]

And he took the children in his arms, put his
hands on them and blessed them *(Mark 10:16)*.

❧

The ministry of Jesus was marked by touching. He was personally involved with people—all kinds of people. Some of them you wouldn't have wanted to touch. Have you ever had an unkempt, dirty, smelly homeless person approach you for money in a shopping mall? Many of us not only refuse to touch such a person, we also draw back. We're repulsed. And that's understandable.

But have you ever wondered how Jesus would have responded to such people? Perhaps we have a clue from Scripture: "A man with leprosy came to him and begged him on his knees, 'If you are willing, you can make me clean.' Filled with compassion, Jesus reached out his hand and touched the man" (Mark 1:40-41).

The point of all this is a simple question: If Jesus were here, in your presence, for what reason would He need to touch you? How do you need to be touched by your Savior?

My son, hear the instruction of your father; reject not nor
forsake the teaching of your mother *(Proverbs 1:8 AMP)*.

W hat can fathers do to be involved with their children in both a unique and lasting way? Here are
some activities dads do or have done.

- A father with five children sets aside one
  hour a week for each of his children. This
  hour is their time alone. And the child is
  the one who decides what they will do,
  whether it's reading, wrestling, playing
  games, or going for a snack.

- One father had his children videotape
  interviews with their aunts, uncles, and
  grandparents. The questions asked during
  the interview all related to the years when
  their dad was growing up.

- Another father tape-recorded the family
  meal during Thanksgiving and Christmas for a number of years. When each
  child married, he gave that child a set of
  the tapes.

What can you do to enhance your parenting role in
your home?

Jesus said to them, "Surely you will quote this proverb
to me: 'Physician, heal yourself!'" *(Luke 4:23).*

W hen you're a parent, a portion of your life is devoted
to camping out in doctors' offices. You listen, follow
their advice, and in many ways you're dependent on them.
But like the rest of us, doctors have limitations, and there
are some diseases and problems they cannot cure.

The title of *physician* was given to Jesus by…Jesus!
And heal He did:

> When evening came, many who were demon-
> possessed were brought to him, and he drove
> out the spirits with a word and healed all the
> sick (Matthew 8:16).

> Great crowds came to him, bringing the lame,
> the blind, the crippled, the mute and many
> others, and laid them at his feet; and he healed
> them (Matthew 15:30).

Don't you wish Jesus were here today to lay His hands
on people around us or perhaps even on you? If you could
ask Jesus to heal you or a family member, what would
you want healed?[141]

You have been a refuge for the poor, a refuge
for the needy in his distress, a shelter from the
storm and a shade from the heat. For the breath
of the ruthless is like a storm driving against a wall
and like the heat of the desert *(Isaiah 25:4-5)*.

You're working out in the backyard. The sun beats down hotter and hotter. You then glance around to see if there's any shade available. You look up to see if there are any clouds in the sky. If there are, you try to figure out if one will drift by and cast its shadow on you. If and when that does happen, you find relief. The only problem is, shadows don't stand still. They move, so you have to move.

Some of life's shadows, however, turn up the heat. Something unexpectedly casts a shadow over your life. And, unfortunately, these shadows tend to stay for awhile. How can we handle these shadows? By shifting ourselves underneath another shadow permanently: "Every good thing given and every perfect gift is from above, coming down from the Father of lights, with whom there is no variation or shifting shadow" (James 1:17 NASB).[142]

You created my inmost being; you knit me together in my mother's womb *(Psalm 139:13)*.

A ren't children a wonder? They can amaze you. Then again, they can frustrate you. They can bring you overwhelming joy or they can break your heart. Above all, they are important—not just to you, but to God.

Your opinion of yourself may fluctuate from time to time, but it probably remains fairly stable. Your children have opinions of themselves too. Perhaps we could call these opinions a mental picture.

As a parent, would you say that the picture you have of yourself matches what God says about you in Psalm 139? What about your children? Do their mental images reflect this in-focus picture? If not, you may want to read Psalm 139:13-18 out loud for a number of days. Let its truths soak into your heart and mind so they will refocus your lens. When you have a clear focus of yourself, then you can help your children have a clearer focus on who they are. Let God's Word be your standard.

[Jesus] said to them, "Let the little children come to me..." and he took the children in his arms, put his hands on them and blessed them *(Mark 10:14,16).*

W hat is the best way to pray for yourself and your children? Sometimes we can get so busy as a parent that prayer is a last-minute thought, a last resort, or is half-finished because we fall asleep in exhaustion. How can you change that?

First, pray when you're fresh and alert. This will vary because of your metabolism. There is no "best time."

Then, when you pray, be specific.

Third, have you ever prayed Scripture passages aloud? Why not try it?

Fourth, keep a prayer journal. Write out some of your prayers in detail. Remember to add the answers to your prayers when you get them.

Fifth, remember to ask God what He wants you to pray about for your children.

Finally, remember that some of the prayers you pray for your children are "future or waiting prayers." Just remember this: "Confess your sins to each other and pray for each other so that you may be healed. The prayer of a righteous man is powerful and effective" (James 5:16).

Become useful and helpful and kind to
one another *(Ephesians 4:32 AMP)*.

The boomerang is a weapon used for hunting in Australia. That's where the boomerang was invented. When a skilled person uses it, the boomerang can be thrown for a great distance. If it misses the target, it circles around and comes back to the hand of the thrower. Amazing? No, not really. That's its purpose. It was constructed to do that.

Our behavior is just like a boomerang. The way we act toward other people will return to us. Most parents begin teaching their children this principle at an early age, especially the boomerang effect of kindness.

Kindness is a character quality that is never forgotten. Your acts of kindness will return to you like a boomerang. It may take awhile—even months—for your kindness to return to you, but be patient. What you do will be remembered. And perhaps someone who doesn't yet know the Lord will ask, "Why are you so kind?" Then you will have an opportunity to tell him or her about Jesus' work in your life.

This is what the LORD says: "Let not the wise man boast of his wisdom or the strong man boast of his strength or the rich man boast of his riches, but let him who boasts boast about this: that he understands and knows me, that I am the LORD, who exercises kindness, justice and righteousness on earth, for in these I delight" *(Jeremiah 9:23-24)*.

The goal of our lives is to understand and know God. And the more you know Him, the more you're able to praise Him. But did you know that works both ways? The more you praise Him, the more you will know Him.

Did you also know there's a difference between praise and thanksgiving? Think about that for a minute. You thank your children at times. And you praise them too. Perhaps both of these are mixed together at times. But when it comes to God, there is a distinction between the two. Dr. Lloyd Ogilvie explains:

> Praise would be distinguished from thanksgiving. When we give thanks, we glorify God for what He has done; when we praise Him, we glorify Him for what He is in Himself. Praise concentrates on God for Himself rather than His gifts and provisions. And according to His own desires expressed so clearly, He longs for us to glory in the fact that we understand and know Him. The depth of our praise measures the quality of our relationship with Him.[143]

Six days you shall labor, but on the seventh day
you shall rest; even during the plowing season
and harvest you must rest *(Exodus 34:21)*.

D o you have a regular time of rest? Real rest? Parents
who are asked this question respond in a variety
of ways. They don't say anything, but look at the ques-
tioner like he's lost his mind. Or they say, "You've got to
be kidding. With three toddlers? Right!" or "Not with
my schedule. It's impossible!" or "I think I did…six years
ago."

Many people feel that rest is not even possible during
the parenting years. But it's got to be there. It's a must
scripturally and physically. It's easy to ignore both the
Sabbath and your own needs. Sometimes you don't even
know you're ignoring your needs because everything you
do is admirable and applauded.

If someone mentions the word *rest* to you, what's the
first thought that comes to mind? Unnecessary, waste,
elusive, deserved? The word *rest* is not in the vocabulary
of workaholics. Many came from homes that equated
rest with laziness. Fortunately God defines rest differently. He sees rest as necessary; He sees it as something
needed so we can worship Him.

Give thanks to the LORD, for he is good; his
love endures forever *(Psalm 107:1)*.

Let us come before him with thanksgiving and
extol him with music and song *(Psalm 95:2)*.

~

Thanksgiving day. Platters of food, mouth-watering aromas, everyone waiting for the first servings—especially the children. Can you imagine what their reaction would be if you gave them a plate with five kernels of corn on it? That's what the pilgrims did when they celebrated the first Thanksgiving. It was done to remind them of the difficult year they had experienced. After prayers of gratitude were offered, then the meal was served.

Think back to the first Thanksgiving you can remember. Try to capture the sights, the sounds, the food, and who was there. Have you ever asked the people at your own Thanksgiving table what they remember about Thanksgivings past?

How can you make your Thanksgiving memorable and different this year? How might your family reflect the true meaning of the occasion?[144]

There is now no condemnation for those who
are in Christ Jesus…If Christ is in you, your body
is dead because of sin, yet your spirit is alive
because of righteousness *(Romans 8:1,10)*.

The following prayer from William Barclay reminds us
of what Jesus did for us and what He will do for us.

> O God, our Father, we thank You that You
> sent Your Son Jesus Christ into this world to
> be our Savior and our Lord.
>
> We thank You that He took our body and
> our flesh and blood upon Himself, and so
> showed us that this body of ours is fit to be
> Your dwelling place.
>
> We thank You that He did our work, that
> He earned a living, that He served the public,
> and so showed us that even the smallest tasks
> are not beneath Your majesty and can be done
> for You.
>
> We thank You that He lived in an ordinary
> home, that He knew the problems of living
> together, that He experienced the rough and
> smooth of family life, and so showed us that
> any home, however humble, can be a place
> where in the ordinary routine of daily life we
> can make all life an act of worship to You.
>
> Lord Jesus, come again to us this day.[145]

> You, then, why do you judge your brother? Or why
> do you look down on your brother? For we will all
> stand before God's judgment seat *(Romans 14:10)*.

～≫

Your partner will do some things that bother you or even hurt you. So will your children. What will you do with those behaviors that leave you with a wound? God's Word has an antidote to your natural response. It's an interesting concept; in fact, it's reminiscent of the three monkeys: "Hear no evil," "See no evil," and "Speak no evil." That's good advice. God's Word adds a fourth suggestion: Think no evil (1 Corinthians 13:5).

Thinking no evil—what a task! It's so easy to think the worst about people. In fact, we all have a bent toward doing that because we've been marred by original sin. It's not our nature to give other people the benefit of the doubt, but God says it's a better way. And it's not our nature to forgive and let another person off the hook, but again God says it's a better way.[146]

Since ancient times no one has heard, no ear has perceived, no eye has seen any God besides you, who acts on behalf of those who wait for him. You come to the help of those who gladly do right, who remember your ways *(Isaiah 64:4-5)*.

Waiting. Some parents feel as though they spend their whole life waiting. Sometimes when we're facing difficult times we feel like we're waiting for God. In fact, sometimes we think He's slow to respond to our needs. Or we think He's simply absent.

We may not feel that God is doing anything to help us with what we're facing. Why? Because we want help *now*. The instant-solution philosophy of society often invades a proper perspective of God. We complain about waiting a few days or weeks, but to God a day is as a thousand years, and a thousand years is as an instant. God works in hidden ways, even when you and I are totally frustrated by His apparent lack of response. Remember the words of today's verses.

God has a reason for everything He does and a timetable for when He does it.

The fruit of the Spirit is love, joy, peace, patience, kindness, goodness, faithfulness… *(Galatians 5:22)*.

⤳

In the parable of the Prodigal Son, the son came to his father and asked for his share of the inheritance. The father could have simply denied his son's request. He could have given the son a part of his inheritance and saved the rest for later. He could have given his son the money but then somehow kept him from leaving. Or, as so many parents do, he could have gone after his son to save his money and rescue him from his evil friends. There are probably other options he could have chosen, but he didn't.

In dealing with his rebellious son, this father did not throw out his value system, his way of life, or his relationship with the rest of the family. Some people might say that the father was too permissive, and he made a mistake giving his son all that money. But let's take a closer look at some of the details in this parable. The father did four things:

- The father let his son go.
- The father was patient.
- The father was forgiving.
- The father was faithful to his rebellious son.

God's faithfulness to us is a worthy model for the relationships between us and our children.

Wait for the LORD; be strong and let your
heart take courage *(Psalm 27:14 NASB).*

❧

It takes courage to be a parent. Why? One reason is
because Christian parents raise their children in a non-
Christian society as members of a chosen minority. Look
at the definition according to *Webster's New World Dictionary:* "the attitude of facing and dealing with anything
recognized as dangerous, difficult or painful instead of
withdrawing from it; the courage to do what one thinks
is right." Consider the words of Tim Kimmel:

> It takes courage to take blame, to admit that we
> are wrong. It takes courage to swallow our pride,
> to fork down banquets of crow, and to submit to
> the consequences...A courageous person faces
> those he has wronged and openly admits he let
> them down...It takes courage...
>
> > ...to be honest.
> > ...to love someone who has hurt you.
> > ...to forgive.
> > ...to confront someone who is wrong.[147]

God's Word puts it this way: "He who conceals his sins
does not prosper, but whoever confesses and renounces
them finds mercy" (Proverbs 28:13). Remember, courage is contagious.

Blessed is he whose help is the God of Jacob,
whose hope is in the LORD his God *(Psalm 146:5)*.

❧

"I'm bored." "I'm not satisfied." "I'm not happy." Complaints. Children voice them, and so do adults. Years ago there were bumper stickers that said "Happiness is…" with many varied answers. Dr. Archibald Hart suggests these principles of happiness:

- Happiness is a choice.
- Happiness is getting your eyes off others.
- Happiness is being able to forgive.
- Happiness is living in the here and now.
- Happiness is appreciating the little things.
- Happiness is keeping your expectations in check.
- Happiness is being yourself.
- Happiness is being able to enjoy pleasure.
- Happiness is wanting the right things.
- Happiness is something you learn.
- Happiness is having the right attitudes.
- Happiness is praying "Thy will be done." This is the prayer to create maturity.[148]

Happiness is… [How will you finish this sentence?]

My command is this: Love each other
as I have loved you *(John 15:12)*.

⌇⌇

Rosalind Rinker is known for her writings on conversational prayer. In one of her works she penned this meditation to remind parents of how to respond to our children.

1. *My child, I love you.*

   I love you unconditionally.

   I love you, good or bad, with no strings attached.

   I love you like this because I know all about you.

   I have known you ever since you were a child…

2. *My child, I accept you.*

   I accept you just as you are.

   You don't need to change yourself. I'll do the changing when you are ready.

   I love you just as you are…

3. *My child, I care about you.*

   I care about every big or little thing which happens to you. Believe this.

   I care enough to do something about it. Remember this.

   I will help you when you need me. Ask me.

   I love you.

   I accept you.

   I care about you.[149]

Be quick to listen *(James 1:19).*

❧

One of the greatest gifts you can give to your child is the gift of listening. As James 1:19 tells us, we are to be ready listeners. Listening is a gift of spiritual significance that you can learn to give to other people. When you listen to others, you give them a sense of importance, hope, and love that they may not receive any other way. Through listening, we nurture and validate the feelings of other people, especially when they are experiencing difficulties in life.

Listening is giving sharp attention to what someone else is *sharing* with you. It's more than just hearing what someone else is saying. Often what people share is more than what they say. We must listen to the total person, not just the words spoken. Listening requires an openness to whatever is being shared: feelings, attitudes, or concerns as well as words. Listening also means putting yourself in a position to respond to whatever is being shared with you.

He who answers before listening—that is
his folly and his shame *(Proverbs 18:13)*.

L istening is an expression of love. It involves caring
enough to take seriously what another person is communicating. When people know you hear them, they will
trust you and feel safe with you. And if you are a good
listener, other people will be more apt to invite you into
their lives. These same people will also learn through
your example to respond openly and lovingly to what
you share with them.

As parents, we need to remember that there is a difference between listening and hearing. The goal of hearing
is to gain content or information for your own purposes.
In hearing, you are concerned about what is going on
inside *you* during the conversation.

With our children, we want to be listeners. We want
to care for and empathize with them. In listening, we
want to understand the thoughts and feelings of our children. We are listening for their sakes, not our own. We
shouldn't think about what we will say when they stop
talking; rather, we should concentrate on what they are
saying.

What do you need to hear from your child today?

Pride goes before destruction, a haughty
spirit before a fall *(Proverbs 16:18)*.

Have you ever been around a person who is so taken with his own importance that he is a legend in his own mind? He is full of pride. Whether it's an adult or a child, eventually you get tired of being around him. Dr. Lloyd Ogilvie shares this about pride:

> We think the opposite of pride is humility. And yet how quickly we become proud of being humble. Pride is a poison that pervades our being. It requires a daily antidote. The purging of the antidote is radical. It begins its work when we confess to God that pride is an idol in our hearts. Then comes the surrender of our lives. But finally only Christ can break the power-bind of pride. It's a miracle of His grace. Pride is really trying to fill our emptiness with self-love. When we experience His unqualified love from the cross and the cleansing power of His blood purges us, only then can we let Him throw down and crush the idol of pride.[150]

> Blessed is the man who trusts in the LORD, whose
> confidence is in him. He will be like a tree planted
> by the water that sends out its roots by the stream.
> It does not fear when heat comes; its leaves are
> always green. It has no worries in a year of drought
> and never fails to bear fruit *(Jeremiah 17:7-8)*.

There is an agony in life that is totally avoidable. It has to do with the feelings that are generated by worry. Why does the Bible have so many verses about worry? Because of the fall of man we all have a bent toward worry, and God wants to help us overcome it.

A blessed man is one who receives something from God. In today's verses, God is promising stability. He wants to give us a worry-free mindset regardless of what is going on with our children, spouse, school, work, and parents. We can choose to look to God or focus on our circumstances.

What could you do to make being worry-free a reality in your life?[151]

Go out at once into the streets and lanes of
the city and bring in here the poor and crippled
and blind and lame *(Luke 14:21 NASB)*.

How do your children respond when they encounter a homeless person? How do you feel when that
poorly dressed person or family holds up a ragged piece
of cardboard that says, "Will work for food"?

The poor and homeless will always be part of our lives.
Yes, *our* lives. Some people are just one step or one bill away
from homelessness. What is our responsibility? Better yet,
what is our attitude? What do our hearts say? It's easy to
judge the homeless and withhold assistance so that we
don't encourage them to continue begging. But do we
know what we could do to help them? Our calling is not
to judge, but to love.

The message in Luke 14 is one of mercy. In what ways
does your family show mercy to other people?

> Then he threw his arms around his brother
> Benjamin and wept, and Benjamin embraced
> him, weeping. And he kissed all his brothers
> and wept over them *(Genesis 45:14-15).*

Joseph knew how to cry. In the family reunions described in Genesis 42–50 we see several instances of crying. Of course, that happens a lot at family reunions, doesn't it? "Deeply moved at the sight of his brother, Joseph hurried out and looked for a place to weep" (Genesis 43:30). Joseph wept again—uncontrollably—when his brother Judah pleaded for Benjamin not to be kept in Egypt so that Jacob would be spared from any more pain (Genesis 45:2).

We also have the record of Joseph weeping when his father arrived in Egypt (46:29), when his father died 17 years later (50:1), and when his brothers sent a message to him asking him to forgive them (50:17).

When Jesus arrived in Bethany following the death of Lazarus, He wept (John 11:35).

When words fail, tears are the messenger. Tears are God's gift to all of us so we can release our feelings.

Pray without ceasing (1 Thessalonians 5:17 NASB).

⤳

"There's never enough time for all I have to do, let alone set aside time to pray. Isn't the apostle Paul asking a bit much when he says to pray unceasingly?" What Paul is really talking about are frequent, brief prayers expressed while we're walking, waiting on a phone call, driving (with eyes open!), or at any other time.

As parents, we need to pray constantly for our children. What can we pray for? Pray for our children's spiritual growth, their character development and any character defects, their views and attitudes about themselves, their ability to say no to temptation, their daily difficulties, the types of friends they will have, protection when they date, and wisdom when they select their partner. But above all, praise God for each of your children—who they are and who they will become.

> When parents truly pray for their offspring, their prayers bind both their soul and the souls of their children into a mystery that ultimately deepens the life of each.[152]

[God said to Solomon,] "I will give you a wise and discerning heart, so that there will never have been anyone like you, nor will there ever be" *(1 Kings 3:12).*

❦

I f God said to you, "Ask Me for anything that you want and I'll give it to you," what would you ask for? Many people would ask for power and control. They believe that will relieve their anxiety. After all, wouldn't we like to have more power and control over our teens?

But asking for wisdom will help you use power in a positive and healthy way. Wisdom will equip you to evaluate your priorities in a way that enables you to use money and not abuse it. Wisdom will help you to discern the needs and requests of your children. When your children ask for something, you may want to say, "Let me consider your request for a while. I want to ask God for His wisdom in making that decision." That may seem like a radical approach, yet it's what God wants from us in all areas of our lives.

The word of God is living and active. Sharper than any double-edged sword, it penetrates even to dividing soul and spirit, joints and marrow; it judges the thoughts and attitudes of the heart *(Hebrews 4:12)*.

❧

I can't change. I've tried and tried. I'm stuck." Many people actually believe those words. They try not to yell at the kids, or blow up, or nag them, but they can't seem to change. Yet God's Word says emphatically that we *can* change.

Change is possible for those of us who are believers in Christ Jesus because our faith is an inward transformation, not just an outward conformity. When Paul says, "My dear children, for whom I am again in the pains of childbirth until *Christ is formed in you,*" he is telling us that we have to let Jesus Christ live *in* and *through* us (see Galatians 4:19).

In Ephesians 4:23 we are told to "be renewed in the attitude of your minds." This means we must give Him access to our memory banks and the past experiences that need to be relinquished.

The word of God is living and active. Sharper than any double-edged sword, it penetrates even to dividing soul and spirit, joints and marrow; it judges the thoughts and attitudes of the heart *(Hebrews 4:12).*

L et's look again at Hebrews 4:12. The word *active* actually means "energize." God's Word *energizes* us for change. How? The apostle Paul says, "We take captive every thought to make it obedient to Christ" (2 Corinthians 10:5). As a child perhaps you played a game called Capture the Flag. As adults, we need to engage in capturing our thoughts. Why? Because that is usually where negative feelings begin and communication problems start.

How can we capture our thoughts? By memorizing Scripture. What thoughts would you like to be rid of today? Write them down. Ask God to make you aware of when those thoughts pop into your mind. Write down the thoughts you would like to have in place of the old ones. Read them aloud several times a day. And watch out—this will put you on the road to change!

Without faith it is impossible to please God,
because anyone who comes to him must
believe that he exists and that he rewards those
who earnestly seek him *(Hebrews 11:6)*.

~~~

Faith is the essence of the Christian's day-to-day activities. Paul wrote, "As you have received Christ Jesus the Lord, so walk in Him" (Colossians 2:6 NASB). How did you receive Christ? By faith. How, then, are you to walk in Him? By faith. In Scripture, walking refers to the way you conduct your everyday life. Thus successful Christian living and spiritual maturity are determined by our belief in God.

We tend to think of faith as some kind of mystical quality that belongs only in the realm of the spiritual. But everybody walks by faith. It is the most basic operating principle of life. The question is, "In what or whom do you believe?" We are challenged to believe in God and take His Word seriously.[153]

In what area would you like more faith? In what area do your children need more faith?

Moses said to the LORD, "O Lord, I have never been eloquent, neither in the past nor since you have spoken to your servant. I am slow of speech and tongue" *(Exodus 4:10).*

W e've all felt like Moses at one time or another. We're asked to do something new or we already have a commitment and we want out. We want to be let off the hook, and we can think of a multitude of excuses just like Moses did. Remember that God had already told Moses that He would be with him. Moses had the assurance that he wouldn't be alone, but he was still afraid.

Sometimes at first we believe we can complete the tasks. Then our minds begin to wander and create worst-case scenarios. These scenarios seem so real they make us afraid. What's the answer? Remembering what God said in Exodus: "I will be with you," and saying, "If God calls me to do something, He will enable me to do it. I'll trust Him and go for it."[154]

Now it is God who makes both us and you stand firm
in Christ. He anointed us, set his seal of ownership
on us, and put his Spirit in our hearts as a deposit,
guaranteeing what is to come *(2 Corinthians 1:21-22)*.

M ost of us can't afford to pay cash for a home or even
a car. We buy houses and cars on time. However,
we still have to save money for the down payment. Once
you sign the documents and hand over the check, you're
into your home. But it's not paid for yet; you'll have payments for years. You can depend on that!

A down payment has been made for you as a believer.
When you accepted the Lord as your Savior, you received
a gift—the Holy Spirit. This represents God's down
payment to you with the promise that He will make
additional payments to you. That's some gift! The Holy
Spirit is also a seal of ownership on you. You are owned
by God, and He promises that you will receive all that
comes with salvation.[155]

You know that we dealt with each of you as a
father deals with his own children, encouraging,
comforting and urging you to live lives
worthy of God *(1 Thessalonians 2:11-12)*.

W hat legacy are you leaving as parents? Each of us is
creating our own legacy right at this very moment.
We have been creating our legacy for many years. As Tim
Kimmel says in his excellent book *Legacy of Love,*

> Your words, your schedule, your choices,
> your obedience, the way you savor your vic-
> tories and the way you swallow your defeats
> all help to define your life. It is this defini-
> tion that your children rely on most as they
> seek to chart their own future.[156]

We don't have any option when it comes to leaving
a legacy. However, we do have an option as to the *kind*
of legacy we leave. What are people receiving from you?
What are you giving to make your family great? And
would you want to hear your eulogy in advance?[157]

I give them eternal life, and they shall never perish; no
one can snatch them out of my hand *(John 10:28)*.

~~~

Pets can bring a lot of enjoyment to the home…as well as some additional work. Most families have at least a dog or a cat. There are lessons to learn from the presence of an animal. Have you ever noticed how a mother cat carries her kittens? She's not like a baby monkey who has to grasp onto his mom with his little paws and hold on for dear life. A kitten doesn't have to hang on; the mother grasps the baby by the neck with her teeth and carries it around. The kitten's security depends on the mother.

What does your security depend upon? What about your child's security? Let's look at your security in your salvation. Does your salvation depend on your ability to hang on like a baby monkey or does it depend on who God is and what He does? What do you believe? Better yet, what does the Scripture teach? Sometimes we let our childhood and life experiences shape what we believe about salvation rather than Scripture. Remember that your spiritual security in Christ is permanent.[158]

I tell you the truth, unless a kernel of wheat falls to the ground and dies, it remains only a single seed. But if it dies, it produces many seeds *(John 12:24)*.

⌇

As a parent, are you sacrificing for your children or investing in them? Parenting is costly in many ways. Aside from the financial outpouring, parenting can cost you energy, time, privacy, emotional drain, freedom... you finish the list.

Some parents tend to concentrate on what they are giving up. They focus on and complain about what they are sacrificing. Some even remind their children of that periodically. "You kids need to remember all that we've sacrificed for you" is a common message. The focus is more upon the parents rather than the children.

Yet some parents don't see children as a sacrifice but rather as an investment or opportunity. When you invest in something you believe that the returns will be of greater value than what you started with. And when you invest in your children you enjoy them, but when you focus on sacrifices you begrudge them.[159]

God so loved the world that he gave his one
and only Son, that whoever believes in him shall
not perish but have eternal life *(John 3:16)*.

⇜✦⇝

God knows how to give. In fact, He's our model for
sacrificial giving. Take a moment and think about
the gifts you've received from people over the years. Can
you remember the first gift you ever received? What about
the best gift? And, ugh, what about the worst gift? Sometimes families who gather for Christmas or a birthday
celebration ask everyone to answer those three questions.
That makes for a hilarious but insightful time.

Let's think about the purpose of a gift. A gift is an item
that is selected with care and consideration. Its purpose is
to bring delight and fulfillment to another person. It is an
expression of deep feeling on the part of the giver; usually
you put much care and effort into selecting a gift.

How will your gift show the person the extent of your
feeling for him or her and how much he or she means
to you?

NOTES

1. Charles R. Swindoll, *Strike the Original Match* (Portland, OR: Multnomah Press, 1980), p. 92.

2. John White, *Parents in Pain* (Downers Grove, IL: InterVarsity Press, 1979), p. 165.

3. Randy L. Carlson, president, Today's Family Life and Parent Talk Radio, *Father Memories* (Chicago: Moody Press, 1992), pp. 201-02.

4. Paul Heidebrecht and Jerry Rohrbach, *Fathering a Son* (Chicago: Moody Press, 1979), pp. 35-36.

5. Gary Smalley and John Trent, *The Blessing* (Nashville: Thomas Nelson Publishers, 1986), adapted from numerous chapters.

6. Pat Hershey Owen, *Seven Styles of Parenting* (Wheaton, IL: Tyndale House Publishing, 1983), p. 15.

7. Charles R. Swindoll, *Living Beyond the Daily Grind* (Dallas: Word, Inc., 1988), p. 203, adapted.

8. Ibid., p. 103, adapted.

9. Ken Gire, *Instructive Moments with the Savior* (Grand Rapids, MI: Zondervan Publishers, 1992), pp. 30-31.

10. Sheila West, *Beyond Chaos* (Colorado Springs: NavPress, 1991), pp. 122-23, adapted.

11. Owen, *Seven Styles of Parenting*, pp. 48-49, adapted.

12. Tim Kimmel, *Legacy of Love* (Portland, OR: Multnomah Press, 1989), pp. 90-91.

13. Anthony Campolo, "The Risks of Being a Parent," in Jay Kessler, Ron Beers, and LaVonne Neff, eds., *Parents and Children* (Wheaton, IL: Victor Press, 1986), pp. 77-79, adapted.

14. Edith Schaeffer, *What Is a Family?* (Old Tappan, NJ: Fleming H. Revell, 1975), pp. 19, 24, 117.

15. Patrick Morley, *Two-Part Harmony* (Nashville: Thomas Nelson Publishers, 1994), pp. 202-03.

16. Schaeffer, *What Is a Family?* pp. 30, 95.

17. Kent and Barbara Hughes, *Common-Sense Parenting* (Wheaton, IL: Tyndale House Publishers, 1995), pp. 117-21, adapted.

18. Tony and Bart Campolo, *Things We Wish We Had Said* (Dallas: Word, 1988), pp. 213-14.

19. Morley, *Two-Part Harmony*, pp. 196-97, adapted.

20. Henry Gariepy, *100 Portraits of Christ* (Wheaton, IL: Victor Press, 1987), pp. 13-15, adapted.

21. J.I. Packer, *Knowing God* (Downers Grove, IL: InterVarsity Press, 1973), p. 37.

22. Max Lucado, *On the Anvil* (Wheaton, IL: Tyndale House Publishers, 1985), pp. 91-92. Used by permission.

23. Archibald D. Hart, *Stress and Your Child* (Dallas: Word, 1992), p. 142, adapted.

24. William Barclay, *A Barclay Prayer Book* (London: SCM Press Ltd., 1990), pp. 56-57, adapted.

25. Hughes and Hughes, *Common-Sense Parenting*, pp. 20-22, adapted.

26. H. Norman Wright and Gary J. Oliver, *Raising Emotionally Healthy Kids* (Wheaton, IL: Victor Press, 1993), pp. 146-48, adapted.

27. David Allen Hubbard, *Is the Family Here to Stay?* (Dallas: Word, Inc., 1971), p. 79.

28. H. Norman Wright, *Recovering from the Losses of Life* (Grand Rapids, MI: Fleming H. Revell, 1991), pp. 10-11, 19, adapted.

29. Jay Kessler, John Beers and LaVonne Neff, eds., *Parents and Children* (Wheaton, IL: Victor Press, 1986), pp. 109-11.

30. Smalley and Trent, *The Blessing*, pp. 36-41, adapted.

31. A.W. Tozer, *The Knowledge of the Holy* (New York: Harper and Row, 1961), pp. 40-43, adapted.

32. Lucado, *On the Anvil*, pp. 69-70. Used by permission.

33. Gariepy, *100 Portraits of Christ*, pp. 23-24, adapted.

34. Archibald Hart, *15 Principles for Achieving Happiness* (Dallas: Word, Inc., 1988), p. 47.

35. Author unknown, from Ronda De Sola Chervin, *A Mother's Treasury of Prayer* (Ann Arbor, MI: Servant Publications, 1994), pp. 134-35. Used by permission.

36. Stuart Briscoe, *The Sermon on the Mount* (Wheaton, IL: Harold Shaw Publishers, 1995), pp. 28-33, adapted.

37. Phillip Keller, *Strength of Soul* (Grand Rapids, MI: Kregel Publications, 1993), pp. 172-77, adapted.

38. Owen, *Seven Styles of Parenting*, pp. 59-60, adapted.

39. Stuart and Jill Briscoe, *Living Love* (Wheaton, IL: Harold Shaw Publishers, 1993), pp. 60-61, adapted.

40. Dennis Rainey, *The Tribute* (Nashville: Thomas Nelson, 1994), p. 273, adapted.

41. Keller, *Strength of Soul,* pp. 13-14, adapted.

42. John Yates, "The Promises to Pray with My Wife," in Bill McCartney, *What Makes a Man* (Colorado Springs: NavPress, 1992), pp. 72-73, adapted.

43. Briscoe, *Sermon on the Mount,* pp. 139-41, adapted.

44. Ibid., pp. 166-69, adapted.

45. Hart, *15 Principles,* pp. 168-69.

46. A.W. Tozer, *The Root of the Righteous* (Camp Hill, PA: Christian Publications, Inc., 1995), p. 16.

47. Joyce Landorf Heatherly, *Changepoints* (Austin, TX: Balcony Publishing, 1992), pp. 124-25.

48. Jeanne Zornes, *When I Prayed for Patience, God Let Me Have It!* (Wheaton, IL: Harold Shaw Publishers, 1995), pp. 68-72, adapted.

49. William Barclay, *The Gospel of Matthew,* vol. 1 (Philadelphia: Westminster Press, 1956), pp. 114-18, adapted.

50. Zornes, *When I Prayed for Patience,* pp. 86-91, adapted.

51. Ibid., pp. 105-09, adapted.

52. Ibid., p. 24.

53. Ibid., pp. 120-26, adapted.

54. Schaeffer, *What Is a Family?* p. 51.

55. Matthew L. Linn and D. Linn, *Healing Memories* (Ramsey, NJ: Paulist Press, 1974), pp. 11-12.

56. Dean Merrill, *Wait Quietly: Devotions for Busy Parents* (Wheaton, IL: Tyndale House, 1994), pp. 22-23, adapted. Used by permission. All rights reserved.

57. Lloyd John Ogilvie, *Climbing the Rainbow* (Dallas: Word, Inc., 1993), pp. 114-19, adapted.

58. Chris Thurman, Ph.D., *If Christ Were Your Counselor* (Nashville: Thomas Nelson Publishers, 1993), pp. 30-37, adapted.

59. Lloyd John Ogilvie, *Lord of the Loose Ends* (Dallas: Word, Inc., 1991), pp. 43-47, adapted.

60. Charles R. Swindoll, *Home, Where Life Makes Up Its Mind* (Portland, OR: Multnomah Press, 1979), p. 13.

61. Myron Chartier, "Parenting: A Theological Model." *Journal of Psychology and Theology,* 6:54-61 (1978).

62. Ogilvie, *Lord of the Loose Ends*, pp. 127-32, adapted.

63. Ibid., n.p., adapted.

64. Rolf Garborg, *The Family Blessing* (Dallas: Word, Inc., 1987), pp. 11-12, adapted.

65. Wright and Oliver, *Raising Emotionally Healthy Kids*, pp. 154, adapted.

66. Lloyd John Ogilvie, *Silent Strength for My Life* (Eugene, OR: Harvest House Publishers, 1993), p. 27, adapted.

67. Ogilvie, *Lord of the Loose Ends*, pp. 12-15, adapted.

68. Ogilvie, *Silent Strength*, p. 218.

69. Keller, *Strength of Soul*, p. 29.

70. Ogilvie, *Silent Strength*, p. 321, adapted.

71. Briscoe, *Sermon on the Mount*, pp. 9-10, adapted.

72. Gariepy, *100 Portraits of Christ*, pp. 55-56, adapted.

73. Ogilvie, *Silent Strength*, p. 243, adapted.

74. Sidney Simon, *Getting Unstuck* (New York: Warner Books, 1988), pp. 175-79, adapted.

75. Carol Kent, *Tame Your Fears* (Colorado Springs: NavPress, 1993), p. 64.

76. Gire, *Instructive Moments with the Savior*, p. 60. Used by permission.

77. Morley, *Two-Part Harmony*, pp. 38, 146-47, 182-83, adapted.

78. Gariepy, *100 Portraits of Christ*, pp. 65-66, adapted.

79. Paul Lewis, *The Five Key Habits of Smart Dads* (Grand Rapids, MI: Zondervan Publishing House, 1994), pp. 65, 73, 75, 87, adapted.

80. Swindoll, *Living Beyond the Daily Grind*, p. 45.

81. Foster Cline, M.D., and Jim Fay, *Parenting Teens with Love's Logic* (Colorado Springs: Pinon Press, 1992), pp. 30-31, adapted.

82. Ronda De Sola Chervin, *A Mother's Treasury of Prayers* (Ann Arbor, MI: Servant Publications, 1994), pp. 89-90, adapted. Used by permission.

83. Quin Sherrer, *How to Pray for Your Children* (Lynnwood, WA: Aglow Publications, 1986), p. 76.

84. Hughes and Hughes, *Common-Sense Parenting*, pp. 25-29, adapted.

85. Lewis, *Five Key Habits*, pp. 15-16.

86. Michael and Stormie Omartian, "Above All Else," © 1987, See This House Music/ASCAP.

87. Henry Gariepy, *Light in a Dark Place* (Wheaton, IL: Victor Press, 1995), pp. 72-73, adapted.

88. Stormie Omartian, *Power of a Praying Parent* (Eugene, OR: Harvest House Publishers, 1995), pp. 13-14.

89. Tim Hansel, "The Importance of Humor" reprinted from Kessler, Beers, and Neff, eds., *Parents and Children*, pp. 105-06.

90. Gary Jackson Oliver and H. Norman Wright, *When Anger Hits Home* (Chicago: Moody Press, 1992), pp. 76-77, adapted.

91. Rudolph Norden, *Each Day with Jesus* (St. Louis: Concordia Publishing House, 1994), p. 150, adapted. Used by permission.

92. Ibid., p. 364.

93. Charles Swindoll, *Growing Wise in Family Life* (Grand Rapids, MI: Zondervan Publishing House, 1988), p. 59. Used by permission.

94. Carl Mayhall, *When God Whispers* (Colorado Springs: NavPress, 1994), p. 40, adapted.

95. Omartian, *Power of a Praying Parent*, pp. 13-14.

96. Charles R. Swindoll, *The Grace Awakening* (Dallas: Word, Inc., 1990), pp. 8-9, adapted.

97. Ibid.

98. Kimmel, *Legacy of Love*, pp. 261-62.

99. Verna Birkey, *Less Stress, More Peace* (Grand Rapids, MI: Fleming H. Revell, 1995), pp. 20-21, adapted.

100. Gariepy, *100 Portraits of Christ*, pp. 72-73, adapted.

101. Norden, *Each Day with Jesus*, p. 83, adapted.

102. John Mark Templeton, *Discovering the Laws of Life* (New York: Continuum, 1994), pp. 22-23, adapted.

103. Campolo and Campolo, *Things We Wish We Had Said*, p. 63.

104. Merrill, *Wait Quietly*, pp. 108-09, adapted.

105. Ibid., p. 42, adapted.

106. Owen, *Seven Styles of Parenting*, pp. 82-89, adapted.

107. Merrill, *Wait Quietly*, pp. 79-80, adapted.

108. Ibid., p. 81, adapted.

109. Ibid., pp. 82-83, adapted.

110. Wright, *Recovering from the Losses of Life*, pp. 148-49.

111. James R. Beck and David T. Moore, *Why Worry?* (Grand Rapids, MI: Baker Book House, 1994), pp. 18-20, adapted.

112. Merrill, *Wait Quietly*, pp. 216-17.

113. Gariepy, *100 Portraits of Christ,* pp. 95-96, adapted.

114. Ibid., p. 96.

115. Neil Anderson with Joanne Anderson, *Daily in Christ* (Eugene, OR: Harvest House Publishers, 1993), February 29.

116. Judith Mattison, "Delight in the Gift," in Chervin, *Mother's Treasury of Prayers,* pp. 103-04, adapted. Used by permission.

117. Devotion and quote by Larry Crabb adapted from Thurman, *If Christ Were Your Counselor,* pp. 14-20.

118. Lee Roberts, *Praying God's Will for My Daughter/Son* (Nashville: Thomas Nelson Publishers, 1993), selected portions, adapted.

119. Hart, *15 Principles,* p. 24, adapted.

120. H. Norman Wright, *Always Daddy's Girl* (Ventura, CA: Regal Books, 1989), p. 195.

121. Jim Goodwin, "The Impossible Is the Untried," in Templeton, *Discovering the Laws of Life,* pp. 31-32, adapted.

122. West, *Beyond Chaos,* pp. 137-41, adapted.

123. Hart, *Stress and Your Child,* p. 224, adapted.

124. Norden, *Each Day with Jesus,* p. 199, adapted. Used by permission.

125. Gariepy, *100 Portraits of Christ,* pp. 89-90, adapted.

126. Richard Exley, *The Rhythm of Life* (Tulsa, OK: Honor Books, 1987), pp. 127, 137.

127. Ogilvie, *Silent Strength for My Life,* p. 276, adapted.

128. Ogilvie, *Lord of the Loose Ends,* pp. 55-57, adapted.

129. Anderson with Anderson, *Daily in Christ,* February 28, adapted.

130. Merrill, *Wait Quietly,* pp. 186-87, adapted.

131. Anderson with Anderson, *Daily in Christ,* April 6, adapted.

132. Swindoll, *Grace Awakening,* pp. 146-47.

133. Templeton, *Discovering the Laws of Life,* pp. 63-64, adapted.

134. Jack and Judith Bolswick, *The Dual-Earner Marriage* (Grand Rapids, MI: Fleming H. Revell, 1995), pp. 171, adapted.

135. Ogilvie, *Silent Strength,* p. 233, adapted.

136. Rudyard Kipling, "Fill Every Unforgiving Moment with Sixty Seconds of Distance Run," quoted in Templeton, *Discovering the Laws of Life,* pp. 59-60, adapted.

137. Hart, *Stress and Your Child,* pp. 66-69, adapted.

138. Author unknown, found in Chervin, *Mother's Treasury of Prayer*, pp. 34-35.

139. Thurman, *If Christ Were Your Counselor*, p. 134.

140. Oliver and Wright, *When Anger Hits Home*, p. 65, adapted.

141. Gariepy, *100 Portraits of Christ*, pp. 93-94, adapted.

142. Joni Eareckson Tada, *Secret Strength for Those Who Search* (Sisters, OR: Multnomah Books, 1994), pp. 33-34, adapted.

143. Lloyd John Ogilvie, *Conversation with God* (Eugene, OR: Harvest House Publishers, 1992), pp. 19-20.

144. Ogilvie, *Silent Strength*, pp. 345-46, adapted.

145. Barclay, *Barclay Prayer Book*, pp. 8-9.

146. Briscoe, *Sermon on the Mount*, pp. 84-85, adapted.

147. Kimmel, *Legacy of Love*, pp. 139-40.

148. Hart, *15 Principles for Achieving Happiness*, adapted.

149. Rosalind Rinker, *Learning Conversational Prayer* (Collegeville, MN: The Liturgical Press, 1992), pp. 12-13.

150. Ogilvie, *Conversations with God*, pp. 32-33.

151. Beck and Moore, *Why Worry?* pp. 26-29, adapted.

152. Hughes and Hughes, *Common-Sense Parenting*, p. 91. Used by permission of Tyndale House Publishers. All rights reserved.

153. Anderson with Anderson, *Daily in Christ*, May 31, adapted.

154. Kent, *Tame Your Fears*, p. 50, adapted.

155. Paul Ennis, *Approaching God* (Chicago: Moody Publishers, 1991), May 18, adapted.

156. Kimmel, *Legacy of Love*, p. 215.

157. Ibid., pp. 199-200, adapted.

158. Ennis, *Approaching God*, August 15, adapted.

159. V. Gilbert Beers, "Parenting: Sacrifice or Investment?" in Kessler, Beers, and Neff, eds., *Parents and Children*, pp. 79, 80, adapted.